Life, Learning, and Community

Concepts and Models
for Service-Learning
in **Biology**

David C. Brubaker and Joel H. Ostroff, volume editors

Edward Zlotkowski, series editor

A PUBLICATION OF THE

AMERICAN ASSOCIATION
FOR HIGHER EDUCATION

Life, Learning, and Community: Concepts and Models for Service-Learning in Biology
(AAHE's Series on Service-Learning in the Disciplines)
David C. Brubaker and Joel H. Ostroff, *volume editors*
Edward Zlotkowski, *series editor*

Opinions expressed in this publication are the contributors' and do not necessarily represent those of the American Association for Higher Education or its members.

About This Publication
This volume is part of AAHE's Series on Service-Learning in the Disciplines. For information about additional copies of this publication or others in the series from other disciplines, contact:
AMERICAN ASSOCIATION FOR HIGHER EDUCATION
One Dupont Circle, Suite 360
Washington, DC 20036-1110
ph 202/293-6440, fax 202/293-0073
www.aahe.org

ISBN 1-56377-018-0
ISBN (18-vol. set) 1-56377-005-9

Contents

Part 3
The Discipline and Beyond

Appendix

About This Series

by Edward Zlotkowski

The following volume, *Life, Learning, and Community: Concepts and Models for Service-Learning in Biology*, represents the 18th in a series of monographs on service-learning and the academic disciplines. Ever since the early 1990s, educators interested in reconnecting higher education not only with neighboring communities but also with the American tradition of education for service have recognized the critical importance of winning faculty support for this work. Faculty, however, tend to define themselves and their responsibilities largely in terms of the academic disciplines/interdisciplinary areas in which they have been trained. Hence, the logic of the present series.

The idea for this series first surfaced late in 1994 at a meeting convened by Campus Compact to explore the feasibility of developing a national network of service-learning educators. At that meeting, it quickly became clear that some of those assembled saw the primary value of such a network in its ability to provide concrete resources to faculty working in or wishing to explore service-learning. Out of that meeting there developed, under the auspices of Campus Compact, a new national group of educators called the Invisible College, and it was within the Invisible College that the monograph project was first conceived. Indeed, a review of both the editors and contributors responsible for many of the volumes in this series would reveal significant representation by faculty associated with the Invisible College.

If Campus Compact helped supply the initial financial backing and impulse for the Invisible College and for this series, it was the American Association for Higher Education (AAHE) that made completion of the project feasible. Thanks to its reputation for innovative work, AAHE was not only able to obtain the funding needed to support the project up through actual publication, it was also able to assist in attracting many of the teacher-scholars who participated as writers and editors. AAHE is grateful to the Corporation for National Service–Learn and Serve America for its financial support of the series.

Three individuals in particular deserve to be singled out for their contributions. Sandra Enos, former Campus Compact project director for Integrating Service With Academic Study, was shepherd to the Invisible College project. John Wallace, professor of philosophy at the University of Minnesota, was the driving force behind the creation of the Invisible College. Without his vision and faith in the possibility of such an undertaking, assembling the human resources needed for this series would have been very difficult. Third, AAHE's endorsement — and all that followed in its wake

— was due largely to then AAHE vice president Lou Albert. Lou's enthusiasm for the monograph project and his determination to see it adequately supported have been critical to its success. It is to Sandra, John, and Lou that the monograph series as a whole must be dedicated.

Another individual to whom the series owes a special note of thanks is Teresa E. Antonucci, who, as program manager for AAHE's Service-Learning Project, has helped facilitate much of the communication that has allowed the project to move forward.

The Rationale Behind the Series

A few words should be said at this point about the makeup of both the general series and the individual volumes. To some, a science such as biology may seem an unusual choice of disciplines with which to link service-learning, since the latter is largely concerned with societal issues. "Natural fit," however, has not been the determinant factor in deciding which disciplines/interdisciplinary areas the series should include. Far more important have been considerations related to the overall range of disciplines represented. Since experience has shown that there is probably no disciplinary area — from architecture to zoology — where service-learning cannot be fruitfully employed to strengthen students' abilities to become active learners as well as responsible citizens, a primary goal in putting the series together has been to demonstrate this fact. Thus, some rather natural choices for inclusion — disciplines such as anthropology and geography — have been passed over in favor of other, sometimes less obvious selections from the business disciplines and natural sciences as well as several important interdisciplinary areas. Should the present series of volumes prove useful and well received, we can then consider filling in the many gaps we have left this first time around.

If a concern for variety has helped shape the series as a whole, a concern for legitimacy has been central to the design of the individual volumes. To this end, each volume has been both written by and aimed primarily at academics working in a particular disciplinary/interdisciplinary area. Many individual volumes have, in fact, been produced with the encouragement and active support of relevant discipline-specific national societies.

Furthermore, each volume has been designed to include its own appropriate theoretical, pedagogical, and bibliographical material. Especially with regard to theoretical and bibliographical material, this design has resulted in considerable variation both in quantity and in level of discourse. Thus, for example, a volume such as Accounting contains more introductory and less bibliographical material than does Composition — simply because there is less written on and less familiarity with service-learning in accounting.

However, no volume is meant to provide an extended introduction to service-learning *as a generic concept*. For material of this nature, the reader is referred to such texts as Kendall's *Combining Service and Learning: A Resource Book for Community and Public Service* (NSEE, 1990) and Jacoby's *Service-Learning in Higher Education* (Jossey-Bass, 1996).

May 2000

Acknowledgments

The authors would like to acknowledge the valuable assistance of the following:

John Armstrong, Brevard Community College, for sharing his students' reflections.

Linda Brubaker, for her support and assistance.

Linda Ostroff, for her ideas, assistance in reviewing and reediting, and her encouragement.

Audreylynette Wood, for her assistance in typing and postediting this monograph. Without her able hands, we would not have been able to complete this project.

— D.C.B. and J.H.O.

Introduction

by David C. Brubaker and Joel H. Ostroff

This volume stands as one of several in a series connecting service-learning to individual academic disciplines. Although the concept and practice of service-learning in higher education have been around for two decades, its presence has been most apparent in teacher education, nursing, and the social sciences. Although there are obvious applications for service-learning in those fields, incorporation of service-learning into natural science courses has not always seemed practical to science instructors. Many have been suspicious of attempts to incorporate experiential learning into courses responsible for a hefty dose of content and scientific skill development. As little as a decade ago, one could count the number of science courses with a service-learning component on the fingers of one hand. In part, this may have been a reflection of how members of the scientific community (both researchers and teachers) perceived their primary civic role in society — namely, as discovering and creating new bodies of knowledge regarding the physical world and transmitting that knowledge to their students in the classroom and the laboratory. Often they viewed interacting with people and issues in the community outside the academy as someone else's responsibility.

In the past five to seven years, there has been a substantial increase in college science courses with a significant service-learning component, largely due to national and regional conferences as well as the financial support of the national Campus Compact and various state Compacts. We see this as a very positive development and are proud to be a part of it. It also reflects an increasing sense within the biology community that researchers, science teachers, and their students must become more directly involved in their communities and not remain detached from the pressing issues that revolutionary discoveries in cellular, molecular, and developmental biology have provided. The need for more understanding of and care for an increasingly degraded natural environment also illustrates the importance of a more effective integration of academic research, general education, and community action. Much of the increase in service-learning–related science courses has been in the fields of biology, environmental science, and environmental health. Although these three areas of study are clearly interconnected, the focus of this volume is on service-learning in biology.

At this point, it seems appropriate to look at a couple of the ways in which service-learning can be defined. This will provide a context for seeing how the authors included here have wrestled with issues such as traditional content and the benefits of experiential learning, the difference between engaging in service-learning and merely providing community service, and how one can best assess the value service-learning adds to participating students' understanding and appreciation of course material as well as their ability to apply that knowledge in real-world circumstances.

The National and Community Service Act of 1990 defines service-learning as an initiative in which:

1. Students learn and develop through active participation in thoughtfully organized service experiences that meet actual community needs and that are coordinated in collaboration with the school and community;

2. The service is integrated into the students' academic curriculum or the service project provides structured time for them to think, talk, or write about what they did and saw during the actual service activity;

3. The service activity provides students with opportunities to use newly acquired skills and knowledge in real-life situations in their own communities; and

4. The service enhances what is taught in school by extending student learning beyond the classroom and into the community and helps foster the development of a sense of caring for others. (Cohen and Kinsey 1994: 5-6)

Or, as another definition puts it:

Service-learning is a teaching methodology [that] links classroom learning and community service to enrich learning experiences and emphasize civic responsibility. Through service-learning experiences, students develop a sense of responsibility for their community and help meet unmet societal needs. (Buchanan 1996)

The articles in this volume provide a diverse array of service-learning courses in biology that demonstrate one or more of the above characteristics. We think they will stimulate thought and encourage biologists to either increase their efforts to incorporate service-learning into their courses or embark upon this educational adventure for the first time. We have organized these articles into three parts plus appendices: Part 1, Service-Learning as a Mode of Civic Education; Part 2, Course Narratives; and Part 3, The Discipline and Beyond.

Part 1 contains two articles that explore why biology departments should engage their students in service-learning. The first article, by John Kennell, explores several aspects of service-learning and why its incorporation into courses and core curricula is important for biologists. Kennell argues that service-learning projects "allow students to experience biology in real-world settings and offer insight into concepts that underlie biological phenomena faced by our society in ways that cannot be adequately provided in the classroom." Some of the specific reasons he discusses for incorporating service-learning into biology courses include:

1. It enhances academic learning;
2. Real-world experiences accentuate the need for understanding underlying biological principles;
3. Students are empowered as teachers;
4. Instructors are able to facilitate independent student learning;
5. Students become aware of a broader range of disciplines and career opportunities; and
6. Students see the need for continued education in science literacy and civic responsibility.

In a section of his article on the philosophy of service-learning, Kennell discusses the difference between traditional community service and service-learning. This is an important distinction, especially for instructors new to service-learning. In the traditional community service model, the community is the sole recipient of a service provided by the student. However, in service-learning there is a powerful reciprocal arrangement. The students and the community are both equally providers and recipients. The essence of this relationship is captured in a principle quoted by Kennell. "I serve in order that I may learn from you."

In the second article, Jeffrey Simmons describes how he uses ecology and environmental science projects as avenues for the integration of service-learning into his courses. Simmons recognizes that students and citizens all have some level of concern for the environment, and that this focus offers an especially wide range of potential project areas in the community. His experience also suggests that service-learning enhances student learning in a variety of ways, including motivation. He discusses how students gain ownership of their education by engaging in service projects that demonstrate the utility of their knowledge. Simmons then identifies a range of projects that have worked for him.

Part 2, Course Narratives, provides a broad spectrum of service-learning course examples. They come from such diverse areas as field botany, watershed analysis, animal behavior, and cell biology and they span a variety of service models, from traditional field-based interventions to the innovative use of live video Internet connections to local high schools. They also illustrate that service-learning can be successful in courses offered at institutions as diverse as small colleges and major research universities. Many of these courses were initially funded through grants either from the national or a state Campus Compact or from the Corporation for National and Community Service's Learn and Serve America: Higher Education program.

Nancy Prentiss, from the University of Maine at Farmington, uses service-learning as an option to the traditional term paper in her Field

Botany course. Her students teach wildflower and fern identification to fourth and fifth graders at a local public school — a project that not only enriches the elementary school students' sense of the natural world but also helps teachers expand their knowledge of the natural sciences.

Marianne Robertson, from Millikin University in Illinois, sponsors a similar project. In her Animal Behavior course, students are required to serve as facilitators of sixth graders' research projects in animal behavior. Her arrangement, well coordinated with the school principal and parent liaisons, allows the elementary students to come to the university to work on their projects with their mentors. At the end of the year, the students present their results at a science fair.

Alan Raflo, from Virginia Tech, shows what can be done with service-learning at a large university. Using the Virginia STEP (Service Training for Environmental Progress) as the springboard for his service-learning projects, he has coordinated more than 40 projects with students who actually live and work in the communities served. These projects have centered around groundwater quality, surface water quality, and landfill and solid waste management, and are conducted as 10-week summer internships. Raflo discusses both the relevance of these projects to his school's biology program and the identifiable learning outcomes achieved by his students.

At Azusa Pacific University, where Scott Kinnes teaches, the institution actually requires students to engage in service projects in order to graduate. Kinnes began his service-learning work through his general biology course, in which students presented laboratory exercises to home-schooled children of Azusa Pacific faculty. In time, this initiative became part of a Biology Community Outreach program where students in his Ecology and 100-level General Biology II courses prepare laboratory exercises for fourth and fifth grade children in the local schools.

Amal Abu-Shakra and Tun Nyein, from North Carolina Central University, won a National Society for Experiential Education award for their "Cascade Model" of service-learning. In their article, they describe the history of their successful program, which incorporates service-learning into both junior/senior-level biology courses and freshman health and wellness courses in the Department of Health Education. After beginning as a service-learning partnership with a local high school, the program quickly expanded to include elementary schools, magnet schools, and community agencies.

Christine Brown and Samuel McReynolds, from the University of New England, demonstrate how one can use service-learning to engage students in the multidisciplinary study of a local watershed. Brown and McReynolds have students from the Department of Life Sciences and the Department of Social and Behavioral Sciences work together in gathering baseline data on the human population and the population of other life-forms in the York

River watershed. By working in multidisciplinary teams, the students break down traditional barriers to communication and learning across disciplines.

Paul Austin, another faculty member from Azusa Pacific, has developed a unique combination of service-learning and current Internet technologies. His first-semester general biology students select one of three laboratory investigations in cellular/molecular biology to present to a class of Advanced Placement students at a local high school. The Azusa students perfect their mastery of the material, create a webpage, and develop presentations. Then they present a lab live over the Internet through interactive video. Austin explains his criteria for demonstrating learning and how he evaluates the effectiveness of this service-learning exercise.

Our last course narrative comes from Peter Lortz, who deals with the challenges of implementing service-learning in biology and biology-related courses at North Seattle Community College. Since many community college students are nontraditional learners and/or bring to their courses significant work and family obligations, getting them to engage in service-learning can pose a special challenge. On the other hand, the majority of community college students come from the same local communities in which their service-learning projects take place. This intimate link with the local community can make service-learning both more personal and more attractive. Lortz explores the different formal arrangements faculty at his college have experimented with, and reaches some tentative conclusions about the factors shaping an effective natural science service-learning program.

Part 3, The Discipline and Beyond, features a multidisciplinary biology-based program as well as a concluding statement by the coeditors. In his article on the Bahamas Environmental Research Center, Luther Brown of George Mason University presents a program that models not only interdisciplinary collaboration but also a full partnership between the academy and the community. Here biology education and biology research are carried out in a complex, flexible, reflective manner rarely characteristic of today's natural science programs but perhaps prophetic of programs to come.

Finally, as this volume's coeditors, we round off its collection of essays with a discussion of why biology as a discipline must move more rapidly to incorporate service-learning in all areas of biology instruction. In the course of this discussion, we stress how important it is that both faculty and students move to embrace a service model in which the academy and the community are truly reciprocal givers and learners. Such a model implies an appreciation of what it means to be a reflective learner, where one learns about oneself from the people one serves *and* about the people one serves as well as the science that frames the overall experience.

Life, Learning, and Community concludes with four appendices. In the first we have reprinted three short course narratives from Campus Compact's 1996 publication *Science and Society: Redefining the Relationship*. A second appendix contains eight even shorter sketches of biology courses with a service-learning component. It is our hope that these two appendices will provide still more ideas for readers interested in incorporating service-learning into biology curricula. The third appendix offers a list of readings useful for those interested in learning more about service-learning. The final appendix provides contact information on the volume's primary contributors.

References

Buchanan, Renee. (April 8, 1996). "Service-Learning and Tenure." Learning Network, Internet.

Cohen, J., and D. Kinsey. (Winter 1994). "Doing Good and Scholarship: A Service-Learning Study." *Journal of Education:* 4-14.

Educational Benefits Associated With Service-Learning Projects in Biology Curricula

by John C. Kennell

Laboratory courses are an integral component of biological science curricula, since they provide a hands-on approach to teaching science. Laboratories not only expose students to the tools, organisms, and methods scientists use to test hypotheses but also help reinforce basic principles described in classroom lectures. In much the same manner, service-learning (SL) projects allow students to experience biology in real-world settings and offer insight into concepts that underlie biological phenomena faced by our society in ways that cannot be adequately provided in the classroom.

For the past two years, I have incorporated SL projects into an introductory course for nonmajors. The course has a standard lecture/laboratory format and an enrollment of approximately 120 students. I initially decided to incorporate a service component because I felt it would help engage students in the biological issues associated with selected service projects. I found that the projects not only were effective in increasing the students' interest in SL-related issues but also had a noticeable effect on class discussions and written assignments.

In short, the incorporation of the SL projects far exceeded my expectations. As a result, I have become a strong advocate for the beneficial role SL projects can play in science curricula and believe they hold great value as an educational tool.

The incorporation of a new pedagogical approach can be a daunting task in any discipline, but for science curricula that already involve time- and effort-consuming laboratory sections, the idea of implementing an additional course component seems improbable, if not impossible. Unless SL projects offer educational opportunities that are not provided for in the standard lecture/laboratory course format, reasons for incorporating SL projects in biology courses are easily outweighed by the need to cover the basic principles of biological sciences.

I will therefore first address the question of why instructors would consider incorporating a service-learning project in their biology curricula and then describe how — with a minimal amount of course modification — I have integrated service-learning projects into an introductory biology class at Southern Methodist University (SMU).

Why Service-Learning in Biology?

The benefits that SL projects provide to the general curricula in the biological sciences are numerous.

Academic learning is enhanced. Studies have shown that combining community service with classroom instruction can enhance the learning process (Markus et al. 1993). In my own experience, students become more interested in the biological issues involved in their projects and are more apt to discuss these issues in class and seek out relevant information in the library.

Real-world experiences accentuate the need for understanding basic principles of biological sciences. Service-learning projects include issues that cannot be adequately covered in a lecture or laboratory. The principles and practical value of basic research are brought to life by direct interactions with members of society who suffer from, or are striving to improve, a variety of biological phenomena. These experiences help illuminate and reframe specific questions research scientists aim to answer and, in turn, help stimulate interest in the principles that underlie these phenomena.

Students are empowered as teachers. When students share their experiences with the class, they reverse the traditional student-teacher dynamic and create alternative learning opportunities. In some instances, the SL projects involve students serving as instructors to elementary and secondary school children, which tends to increase the students' interest in understanding the scientific principles they describe.

Instructors become facilitators for students to learn independently. The SL projects enable students to learn on their own and in their own way. This changes the role of the instructor from being an information provider to a learning facilitator (Howard 1993). SL projects offer different ways of viewing contemporary issues involving biological science, and students frequently return from service experiences with a number of specific questions. In the model I use in my course, students are able to explore the answers to these questions as part of a required library research report and are encouraged to share their findings in classroom discussions.

Students are made aware of the range of disciplines and different career opportunities associated with biological sciences. A traditional educational goal of many biology courses is to prepare students for careers in medicine or in research-based fields. Alternative career opportunities are often not adequately addressed, despite the expanding role that biologists play in our society. Through interactions with the staff and volunteers at community agencies, students are exposed to a number of professionals who have careers associated with a wide variety of areas that involve biological science.

The projects underscore the need to increase the level of scientific literacy, education, and civic responsibility in our society. Students' views concerning contemporary biological issues, such as society's role in the care of the elderly or policies that regulate human reproductive rights or the environment, are often modified by their SL experiences. It is not uncommon for students to express a great deal of uncertainty about their service projects, and many are forced to reevaluate their preconceived notions of particular groups or individuals in the community. The uncertainty and range of students' responses enable instructors to emphasize the value of providing educational opportunities for all members of our society and the need to increase our nation's level of scientific literacy. An additional benefit of these projects is that they can increase the student's sense of civic responsibility and often serve as a catalyst for additional community service.

Furthermore, through my work with SL projects in an introductory course for nonmajors, I have found that such projects are particularly meaningful for students whose primary field of study lies outside the sciences. Specifically, service projects help engage these students in biological issues that they often have little interest in understanding or to which they have had little exposure. SL projects add a human dimension to issues that often seem irrelevant to the life of the average college student. In addition, such projects help students gain an appreciation for the methods, complexity, and goals of scientific research. In many instances, having a positive experience outside the classroom can invigorate a student who does not have an aptitude for science and can stimulate his or her interest in the course content.

Many of these same benefits undoubtedly apply to students who are majoring in biology. Students who pursue careers in medicine are often motivated by a desire to become primary care givers. SL projects broaden their perspective on the role that biologists and health-care workers play in the community and can help students define their career goals. Exposing biology students to nontraditional career professions associated with some SL projects may also help increase the retention of students who are interested in other areas of biology or are not likely to attend medical school.

A number of recent articles address the value of integrating service into academic courses and discuss additional benefits not identified above (e.g., Giles and Eyler 1994; Howard 1993). Many of these articles are directed at courses in the humanities and often entail lengthy service projects that are a major focus of the course curricula. The model I have used in a large introductory biology class involves a single service experience that does not interfere with the lecture or laboratory schedule. Although the benefit the service provides the community is limited by having students engage in only a single experience, these projects do offer significant value to the course.

Furthermore, such one-shot projects are easier for the instructor to implement than those of larger scope, and they can be incorporated with minor disruption of traditional course content. Before describing the specific projects I have implemented and offering some suggestions regarding the most effective ways to incorporate SL projects into the curricula, we first need to clarify what it is we mean by "service-learning" and how we can distinguish it from both *experiential learning* in general and *voluntarism*.

Philosophy of Service-Learning

Experiential education, the basis of laboratory exercises, aims to engage the learner directly in the phenomena being studied. Service-learning is an extension of experiential learning that involves activities that meet an identified community need and include evaluations of the service in an academic setting. The primary difference between service-learning and voluntarism is that the emphasis of voluntarism is on the service being provided and the intended beneficiary is the recipient, whereas with service-learning both provider and recipient benefits are stressed. In service-learning, the primary benefit to the recipient is the service, and the provider benefits by gaining a broader understanding of and appreciation for the course content — a didactic that has powerful learning outcomes.

Robert Sigmon (1979) has identified the major principles of service-learning as (1) those being served control the services provided, (2) those being served learn to serve and be served by their own actions, and (3) those who serve are learners and have significant control over what is expected to be learned. The reciprocity of this process is best described in the axioms "I serve in order that I may learn from you" and "You accept my service so that you can teach me." Appropriately incorporated into the classroom, SL projects augment course content. Furthermore, their educational outcomes can be incorporated into the same learning cycle (Kolb 1984) that is the foundation of inquiry-based laboratory exercises.

It is important to adhere to the academic principles of service-learning in order to achieve maximum benefit from implementing service components in the curricula. The primary principle is that *academic credit is for learning and not service* (Howard 1993). The incorporation of SL projects should not compromise academic rigor, and students should be fully aware of the way in which they will be evaluated prior to carrying out their projects. In some models, the service projects are mandatory and students accept the service component as a course requirement. In other models, such as the one described below, students are given an alternative and are not required to participate in the SL projects.

Service-Learning in Introductory Biology Courses for Nonmajors

I have incorporated five different service-learning projects and one experiential education project in an introductory biology course entitled The Essentials of Biology. This course provides an introduction to the major concepts of biology for the nonscience major and covers the diversity and interdependence of organisms, with an emphasis on inheritance and evolution. The course includes three hourly lectures and a two-hour laboratory per week, with the lecture and laboratory grades counting for 70 percent and 30 percent of the final grade, respectively.

In addition to standard lecture- and laboratory-based requirements, library research reports and discussion sessions are included that deal with contemporary issues in the biological sciences. In the first week of class, students are given a choice between doing a service-learning project or a library research report. In either case, they must write a two-page report concerning a biological issue; however, those who undertake a service project are not required to include as many citations of primary sources. By offering students a choice, this format establishes that the SL projects are clearly elective. However, even though the projects often involve a greater time commitment than the library research reports, more than 90 percent of the class generally chooses the projects (the percentage represents an average of two semesters, $n = >200$). A further advantage of having two distinct options is that such an arrangement makes it easier to accommodate students who fail to complete their elected service, since those students can be reassigned to carry out library research reports.

Although the nature of each SL project is different, projects are integrated into the course in a similar manner. Students are able to share their experiences with the class during classroom discussions, and credit for the service assignment is based on the quality of the resulting two-page research report. The assignment is worth 15 percent of the lecture grade (10.5% of the total), and its primary goal is to have students acquire the ability to identify primary sources. Although the SL projects reinforce topics discussed in the classroom, questions concerning specific concepts associated with the projects are usually not included on examinations, as the students do not all participate in the same project. Most projects require approximately three to five hours to complete and typically take place on Saturdays throughout the semester. Thus, they do not interfere with the lecture or laboratory schedule. I usually cap the number of students participating in a given project at 20; however, in some cases I expand the number that can participate, since students are able to provide service at different times during the semester. (The specific assignment is reproduced at the end of this chapter.) What follows are brief descriptions of typical SL projects.

• *Serve dinner and entertain residents at a residential facility for HIV+ individuals.* Students must plan a meal and purchase supplies prior to the planned event. Once they arrive at the facility, the students warm the meal they have prepared ahead of time, serve the meal, and eat with the residents. After the meal, students provide some sort of entertainment. In the past two years, this has included having an impromptu jam session and showing a rented video.

• *Perform a service at a local nursing/retirement home.* Students meet with the volunteer coordinator of the home to learn about the facility and how to conduct themselves when interacting with elderly residents. The students organize and participate in a group activity, then are asked to help the residents back to their rooms, where they can spend time asking the residents about their lives, health, and family.

• *Demonstrate laboratory exercises to students who visit the SMU campus.* The SMU athletic department has developed an outreach program, SMU at Your Service, that offers Dallas elementary and middle school children a chance to spend a day on campus. The children tour the campus, attend an athletic event, and participate in demonstrations that have been arranged by members of the SMU faculty and student organizations. These include a magic show presented by students in the chemistry club, informal concerts performed by students in the music department, and laboratory demonstrations carried out by students in my class. Our demonstrations involve setting up several stations in the teaching laboratories with a range of biological organisms and experiments. My students serve as teachers and describe the display or experiment to the children and answer their questions.

• *Serve as guides at a local environmental center.* Students meet with the staff at an environmental education facility supported by the Dallas school district. Following a brief orientation that explains the purpose of the center and provides a description of the nature trails, the students serve as guides to groups of children who visit the center.

• *Entertain seriously ill children who stay at the Ronald McDonald House.* Students spend several hours at a local Ronald McDonald House entertaining children and interacting with their families.

Effectiveness of the SL Projects

Prior to incorporating SL projects into the course curriculum, I devoted four lecture dates to the discussion of contemporary biological issues that relate to topics covered in the course. I now use these sessions to incorporate into the class the students' experiences with their SL projects and, in doing so, am able to observe the effect their projects have on their interest in and knowledge of the biological principles that underlie their service work. These sessions are interspersed throughout the semester and usually follow a group of lectures that relate to the topics being discussed (e.g., a discussion of infectious diseases follows general lectures about viruses, bacteria, and AIDS; see the Course Lecture Schedule reproduced at the end of this chapter). The students who participate in SL projects that relate to these issues (e.g., service at an HIV+ residential facility) must hand in their reports prior to this class and are told that they may be called on to discuss their experiences and describe some of the information they discovered in their research. In previous years when I did not incorporate SL projects into the curricula, it was often difficult to initiate meaningful discussion of certain issues, such as the plight of AIDS patients or the need for immunization programs. Implementation of SL projects has made it significantly easier to get the students to start a discussion, since many of them are eager to tell their classmates of their service experiences. This has helped to stimulate conversations that help reinforce some of the principles that are described in the lectures. A striking aspect of some of these discussions is how, on certain occasions, students have been able to capture the attention of their peers by conveying a particularly meaningful observation or experience they had while performing their service. Their commanding statements often intensify the atmosphere in the classroom and lead to more in-depth discussions of the issue at hand.

An even more significant impact of the SL projects is the effect they have had on the research reports. Students write short library research reports on specific topics selected from four broad areas that cover a number of contemporary issues in biology (i.e., infectious disease, genetic technologies, reproductive rights, and environmental issues). In the two years following the incorporation of service projects, the general quality of the reports has increased, and students who perform a service project tend to carry out library research on very specific issues and are more apt to seek out relevant information. Although these students are not required to incorporate as many citations to primary sources, they often go into greater depth in their research and include more citations in their reports than do the students who have not performed service.

Year-end evaluations show that more than 90 percent of the students who participated in the SL projects felt that the service helped them describe the particular issue they researched, and more than 75 percent thought that their projects made the research more interesting and hence led them to dig a little deeper into the literature. Evaluations also indicate that students have a very positive attitude toward the projects in general, and nearly 100 percent have indicated they were glad they had participated and would recommend the projects to other students in upcoming years.

Almost all of the students who participated felt the SL projects offered a different way of viewing the biological topic involved, and all but one thought they had learned more from the class by participating in a service-learning project than they would have if they had spent more time in the classroom. It is interesting that approximately two-thirds of the students who signed up for the library research projects wished that they had participated in the SL projects, despite the fact that many felt that the SL projects demanded more time than was required to carry out the library research report assignment.

How Do I Go About Integrating SL Projects Into the Curriculum?

I myself benefited greatly from information provided by SMU's Office of Volunteer Services and the experiences of colleagues in other disciplines who had already established contacts with several service agencies. The following guidelines have been invaluable:

• Establish learning goals for the SL projects and ways that students will be assessed.

• Locate agencies that meet the course's educational needs.

• Contact agencies several weeks before the start of the semester to identify a date and task for the project.

• Make the agencies aware of the academic goals involved in the projects so they provide the most meaningful experiences for the students.

• Include the projects on the syllabus and require the students to sign up for the project of their choice within the first few weeks of the semester.

• Include directions to the agency, the name and number of a contact person, and any liability forms that the agencies (or university) may require.

• Have the agencies take attendance.

• Make it clear to the students what they are required to do if they do not fulfill their service obligation.

• Follow up on the projects by asking both the students and agencies whether there are ways to make the projects more meaningful.

The types and number of agencies that are available for service-learning could be constrained at colleges and universities that are located in rural settings, but for the most part, instructors are limited only by their imagination and creativity. Southern Methodist University is nestled in an affluent suburb of Dallas and is protected from some of the problems that plague large cities. Consequently, the average SMU student often has had little exposure to individuals affected by some of the biological phenomena described in class, such as HIV and AIDS or malnutrition. I have specifically designed my projects to provide exposure to these problems. There seems to be an unlimited number of agencies that need assistance, and all the agencies I have dealt with have been eager to have college students participate.

In most cases, the agencies are willing to modify the tasks they would like to have accomplished in order to provide a meaningful experience for the students, and I usually ask that my students be given opportunities to interact directly with the residents they serve. Once suitable agencies have been established, the time needed to prepare for projects in later semesters is reduced significantly.

As I noted above, it is especially important that students understand that they are not being evaluated on the service they perform. Rather, credit is awarded for how well they carry out the report assignment. In my class, reports are scored primarily by number, relevance, and quality of the primary sources cited in the paper. In many instances, it is clear that students have had a truly memorable and meaningful experience at the agency, but if they fail to spend the necessary time in the library carrying out their research, they receive a poor score on their assignment.

Obstacles to Service-Learning Projects in Biology

A worthy goal of SL projects is to allow students to learn from their community service in the same manner they learn in the classroom (Howard 1993). In practice, however, this can lead to problems in disciplines that are based on the dissemination of factual information. It is not uncommon for students to be exposed to opinions that are not based on accurate information or that conflict with ideas presented in class. For example, in an experiential project involving a discussion with the director of a pro-life clinic, my students were told that the rhythm method of birth control is just as effective as birth control pills at controlling unwanted pregnancies. I chose not to correct the speaker. However, I had the opposing speaker from a pro-choice clinic clarify this point when she spoke the following week. Obviously, this could not have been done had the order of visits been reversed, but another tactic I use is to suggest that the students choose as a topic for their library report a controversial point that was brought to light during their project. One student chose to find out whether having an abortion increases a woman's risk of breast cancer, as was stated by the director of the pro-life clinic. She found several recent studies that contradicted his statement, and we discussed these findings in class. It served as an excellent example of the need to make informed choices when it comes to decisions that affect one's health and well-being.

In general, I do not feel that there are any specific obstacles that limit the use of SL projects in the biology curricula, and, in many ways, biology courses have certain advantages over other disciplines due to the wide range of available service opportunities that involve aspects of biological science.

Measuring the Effectiveness of Projects

Assessment of the effectiveness of any new educational technique is always challenging. In my case, I have been able to compare two semesters without the projects with two semesters into which SL projects have been incorporated. The impact that the projects have had on student performance on lecture or laboratory exams has been negligible, mainly because my examinations do not directly include information related to issues associated with the projects. However, as described above, the impact these projects have had on classroom discussions and reports has been remarkable. During my first two years teaching this course, we often had very heated discussions of controversial subjects such as abortion and euthanasia. Following the incorporation of the SL projects, these discussions have been just as heated, but they have often taken different directions because the students participating in SL projects have spoken with much greater conviction and have been able to back up many of their statements with facts researched in the library. They have served, in some respects, as classroom experts and have been able to capture the attention of their peers in ways that an instructor cannot. For example, they have reported firsthand conversations with people afflicted with AIDS and have described the costs and side effects of the drugs these individuals take on a daily basis. They have been able to explain what it is like to live with Alzheimer's disease. One group was astonished to learn that children from underprivileged communities in Dallas often received better training in science classes than they had. In short, the students have illuminated issues that they themselves had questions about prior to their service experiences. Whereas in the first two years I often had to lead discussions alone, I later found that the students who had participated in the service projects would frequently take over a conversation and thus allow me to serve more as a moderator than a lecturer.

I should also note that written reports often include anecdotal accounts that exemplify the positive effect these projects have had on students in the course. Several students have reported that their experiences dramatically altered the way they view a particular group in our society or their opinions on a controversial biological issue. Statements such as "rewarding," "opened my eyes," "made me more comfortable to be around," and "helped me understand" are frequently dispersed throughout the reports, and many students return to the agency they visited to provide additional service.

However, although the SL projects have served as an excellent educational tool, their outcome has not always been predictable. On one occasion, for example, a group of students went to the Dallas Ronald McDonald House and found that there were only three children spending the night there. Consequently, some of the students had little to do. They were understandably disappointed with their project, and this was reflected in a few negative evaluations. Two additional groups went to the same facility later in the semester (over spring break when there are more children staying at the house), and everyone involved reported having had a meaningful experience.

It is, in short, impossible to anticipate all potential problems, and instructors have to be prepared to expect the unexpected. For example, during a student visit at the HIV+ residential facility this semester, one of the residents died. This had a powerful effect on some of the students who were in attendance. However, what could have been a traumatic experience for them turned into a positive educational opportunity as we discussed the death of this individual in class the next day and described how the residents of such facilities have to cope with loss on a daily basis. The value of incorporating these real-world situations into an academic setting is immeasurable.

There is, however, one variable that seems to be more or less consistent: The overall impact of the experiences on participating students is related to the value of the services provided. It is projects that meet a genuine community need that frequently have the greatest impact on the students. The highest percentage of affirmative responses to a question about whether their experiences would make them more active in community service has come from groups who also felt that they had provided a necessary service (i.e., AIDS hospice, nursing home, and Ronald McDonald House). Whether the same association holds true for the students' understanding of the biological phenomena that underlie these projects is a worthwhile subject for future assessment.

Summary

Incorporation of service-learning projects into an introductory biology course for nonmajors has created meaningful opportunities to educate students about biological phenomena faced by members of our society. The model described here involves a single community service visit that does not require significant changes in course content or schedule. The SL projects had a noticeable effect on the level of participation of the students in classroom discussions and led to significant improvements in the quality of library research reports. These findings demonstrate the value of service-learning as an educational tool in biology curricula and provide additional evidence of how community service can impact learning outcomes. SL projects are well suited for nonmajors courses, as they help students understand the impact that science has on individual lives and the local community. In courses for biology majors, SL projects can have similar positive effects by allowing instructors to expand the range of topics explored in laboratory exercises to include those that deal with real-world issues. In this way, they can help students appreciate the broader context of their chosen field of study.

Acknowledgments

I would like to thank Rebecca Bergstresser, coordinator of SMU's volunteer services, for her suggestions, insight, and thoughtful criticism of this piece.

References

Giles, D.E., and J. Eyler. (1994). "The Impact of the College Community Service Laboratory on Students' Personal, Social, and Cognitive Outcomes." *Journal of Adolescence* 17: 327-339.

Howard, J. (1993). "Community Service-Learning in the Curricula." In *Praxis I*, edited by J. Howard, pp. 3-12. Ann Arbor, MI: OCSL Press, University of Michigan.

Kolb, D.A. (1984). *Experiential Learning: Experience as the Source of Learning and Development*. Englewood Cliffs, NJ: Prentice-Hall.

Markus, G.B., J.P.F. Howard, and D.C. King. (1993). "Integrating Community Service and Classroom Instruction Enhances Learning: Results From an Experiment." *Educational Evaluation and Policy Analysis* 15: 410-419.

Sigmon, R. (1979).."Service-Learning: Three Principles." *Synergist* 8: 9-11.

Service-Learning Projects and Library Research Report Assignments

Everyone is required to write a short report that will count for 15% of your lecture grade. There are two basic formats that can be chosen for the Reports: 1) Service-learning project, or 2) Library research report. In either case, you are required to write a report of approximately 2 pages and will be expected to cite several primary sources of information. Certain report topics may be discussed in class during one of DISCUSSION classes that will take place on specific Friday's throughout the semesters. The standard lecture format will replaced on these dates with a 50 minute discussion of contemporary issues in biology. The format for these classes will usually include a 10 minute introduction into the particular topic, followed by an informal discussion of some relevant issues concerning biological sciences. During the discussion of your chosen topic, you may be called upon to answer general questions concerning your project or paper.

Purpose: The objective of this assignment is to make you familiar with biological issues that affect people in our community and to help you learn how to find pertinent scientific information from the variety of scientific information sources that are available in the library and on the Internet. It is hoped that you will develop the skills involved in finding relevant and up-to-date information, which could someday be useful in making decisions that affects your own well-being. A specific objective is to help you identify PRIMARY sources of information from which you can make knowledgeable choices and opinions.

Procedure: You will be asked to sign up for your choice of a service-learning project or library research. There are six different service-learning projects that you can choose from- each one requiring approximately 3 to 5 hours on a specific date arranged by your trusty instructor. If you are unable to attend any of the projects or miss the specific project that you have signed up for, you will need to complete the assignment for a library research project.

Service-Learning Projects

1. AIDS hospice
> Task: Help cook and serve a meal to a group of HIV+ individuals at a facility run by the AIDS services of Dallas
> Requirements: Must meet for a group orientation to plan a meal and entertainment for the event. On the night of the event, you must find transportation to the site, follow the check-in procedures and instructions of the coordinators. If you have a cold or other communicable disease, you cannot attend and will have to do a library research report.
> Reports: You should describe the activity you did at the hospice and how this changed, altered or reinforced your view on the care and treatment of HIV+ individuals (use approximately 1 page). You should also go to the library and find at least one scientific journal article and at least two additional articles that describe a biological issue that it is relevant to AIDS and/or HIV. For example, you might want to find some information on the types of drugs available to inhibit HIV replication, the cost or side-effects of these drugs, issue concerning health insurance for AIDS patients, or how society supports AIDS treatments both locally and world-wide. You may wish to incorporate your experience at the AIDS center with the subject you research.

2. Nursing/Retirement Home
> Task: Perform a service for the elderly at the Juliette Fowler Home. This will likely involve reading, playing a game, or helping with some group activity.
> Requirements: Spend a few hours at the Juliette Fowler Home. You must be able to arrange transportation to and from the site.

Reports: You should describe the activity you did to provide a service at the retirement home and how this changed, altered or reinforced your view on aging or the care of the elderly (approximately 1 page). You should also go to the library and find at least one scientific journal article and at least two additional articles that describe a biological issue that it is relevant to the aging process. For example, you might want to find some information on health care for the elderly, Alzheimer's disease, the importance of physical and mental activity to keeping the body and mind young, or euthanasia. You may wish to incorporate your experience at the retirement home with the subject you research.

3. Woman's Clinic

Task: To meet with the director of the White Rose Woman's clinic and the director of the South St. Woman's Clinic.

Requirements: Group orientation with me, then two separate 2-hour meetings with the directors of the clinics.

Reports: You should describe how your discussion with the Directors of two Woman's clinics changed, altered or reinforced your view on the reproductive rights of women (approximately 1 page). You should also go to the library and find at least one scientific journal article and at least two additional articles that describe a biological issue that it is relevant to reproductive issues. For example, you might want to find some information on abortion alternatives, late-term abortions, RU486, health insurance covering the cost of reproductive procedures, or whether medical students should be taught how to perform abortions. You may wish to incorporate some of the issues that were raised during the discussion with the subject you research.

4. Laboratory Demonstrations

Task: To guide a group of elementary school children through the teaching laboratories in the basement of Fondren Science and help demonstrate some simple laboratory exercises.

Requirements: Must meet for an orientation session with me and be able to participate in two laboratory demonstrations.

Reports: Your report should describe your experience with the children and why you think it is important that they develop an appreciation for science (especially biology) at an early age (approximately 1 page). You should also go to the library and find at least one scientific journal article and at least two additional articles that describe a biological issue that these children would benefit from understanding the underlying biological process. For example, you might want to talk about the importance of hygiene in preventing the spread of bacterial diseases, washing of fruits, ways to prevent getting colds and flu, why you don't want to get sunburned, or the dangers of smoking cigarettes. You may wish to incorporate these issues into a discussion of the role that science education plays in society.

5. Environmental Education Center

Task: Visit the Dallas Independent School District Center for Environmental Education and help guide elementary students on a tour of the facilities.

Requirements: Arrange for transportation to the DISD Environmental Center and spend a some time receiving an orientation before helping to lead a group of elementary or middle-school children on a tour.

Reports: Your report should describe your experience with the children and why you think it is important that they develop an appreciation for our environment at an early age (approximately 1 page). You should also go to the library and find at least one scientific journal article and at least two additional articles that describe a biological issue that these children would benefit from understanding the underlying biological process. For example, you might want to talk about the importance of recycling, limiting energy use, conserving natural resources, maintaining biological diversity or increasing natural habitats. You may wish to incorporate these issues into a discussion of the role that science education plays in society.

6. Ronald McDonald House

    Task: Entertain seriously ill children that stay at the Ronald McDonald House.

    Requirements: Spend a few hours with the children and their families at the Ronald McDonald House.

    Reports: Your report should describe your experience with the children (approximately 1 page). You should also go to the library and find at least one scientific journal article and at least two additional articles that describe a biological issue that relates to the ailments any of the children was experiencing. For example, you might want to research leukemia or other devastating cancers.

Library Research

Task: Pick a topic related to one of the general areas described below (some suggestions are provided), find relevant references to research that has been carried out on the subject, and write a two-page report that incorporates your findings. .

Requirements: To find at least five primary reference sources taken from scientific journal articles, incorporate them into your report and include a bibliography.

DISCUSSION 1 - Infectious Disease
- What have been the most successful strategies at slowing the spread of AIDS
- What is the Ebola Virus? Where do emerging viruses come from and how can they be avoided?
- What are some bacterial diseases that are of major concern? How are they controlled?
- Why are antibiotic resistant strains arising at such a high frequency?
- What are some major protist or fungal infectious diseases? How are they controlled?

DISCUSSION 2: Genetic Technology: Uses and Abuses
- Describe an inherited disease and whether you would you want to be genetically tested
- Should genetically engineered crops be sold? Do they need special labels?
- Describe the pro's and con's of a specific genetic technique
- Describe the procedures involved in DNA fingerprinting and whether it should be admissible in court
- Discuss whether insurance companies should have the right to genetic information

DISCUSSION 3: Reproductive Rights and Right to Die: Abortion, "human cloning", In vitro fertilization, euthanasia
- Describe some current forms of contraception (i.e. RU486, Morning after pill, etc..)
- What are late-term abortions and should they be legal?
- To what extent should your health insurance pay for fertility treatments?
- What is in vitro fertilization? Should you be able to select specific embryos?
- Should "cloning" of humans be allowed?
- Should we be allowed to terminate our own life?

DISCUSSION 4: Environmental Issues
- Dangers using genetically engineered crops or eating genetically engineered foods
- Should the government regulate; air, water, trash, grazing on National Park land, endangered species, environmental policy of third world countries, radon, ozone, chlorine, tobacco smoke, marijuana, bioengineered products etc...?
- Global issues- should we demand developing countries follow our standards?
- Global warming, deforestation, pollution

Report Formats (for ALL reports)

The reports are not to be more than 2 pages in length and are expected to provide a well researched discussion of the biological issue. It is much easier to pick a very specific topic and to give precise details about the research that concerns the topic. Remember, 2 pages maximum for the text (can be single-spaced, but must use at least 12 point font, and have 1" margins on all sides). Don't worry if you haven't followed the format exactly, I'm much more concerned with how well you back up your statements with references and the quality of the references you find. Your reports should be based on facts obtained from Primary Reference Sources.

What is a Primary Reference Source? This refers to an article, research report or published manuscript that describes a research study. Most scientific reports will include a short Introduction which describes the question or hypothesis that is under investigation, Materials and Methods used in the research, Results of the studies and a Discussion of the significance of the findings. Often these reports are very specific, containing charts, graphs and figures and may include scientific jargon that you probably will not be familiar with. Scientific reports are almost always reviewed by a group of scientists prior to publication ("peer-reviewed"), which gives the findings added credibility. One of the hallmarks of science is that the experiments that were carried out are described in such detail that other scientists can repeat the same experiments. This ensures that false claims are not easily made since someone may repeat the experiment. Consequently, the author's reputation is always on the line and his or her statements must be factual.

There is an incredible number of very specific journals which publish scientific research results. There are also a number of journals that review the vast amount of information and present articles that provide a summary of information described in the primary reference sources. In most cases, these review articles provide a citation for each specific point raised so the reader will know where to find the original data. When you read an article in a magazine or in the paper that does not include these citations, you must assume that the author has properly assimilated the information and is describing the facts correctly. In many cases, you can trust the writer's facts, especially in reputable magazines or newspaper; however, there is an alarming amount of misinformation in press and on the WWWeb. Your task is to write a short report on an issue and provide the appropriate citations for each specific point you raise.

Where do I find the Primary Reference Sources? To find the research articles related to your issue, the easiest way is to use the Wilson CD-ROM system that I will describe in class. This is available at the Science and Engineering Library and the library staff can assist you in your search for information but I would like you to do most of the searches on your own. You may use information obtained from the WWWeb, but you must be sure the information comes from a reliable source (and you still MUST include citations to journal articles). In most cases, you'll be primarily interested in articles that appear in journals, and NOT books. Books can be a good place to decide which topic to choose, as are Newspaper articles, and articles from periodicals such as Time or Newsweek; however, your grade on these reports will mainly be based on the number and quality of primary reference sources you include and manner in which you cite the sources in the report. A list of references of unlimited length should be included at the end of your report (but not part of the 2 page limit) and should indicate the source of the each citation (see format below). To document access to the Internet, include the Web site address.

How to make citations: In the text, put "(1)" after a reference to a particular point, and on a separate page list the literature cited in order of its appearance. Follow this format:

> (# in order of appearance in text) Author's last name first, then initials (if more than 3 authors, put the first author and "et al.") (Year of publication) Title of article. Journal name. Volume #: Page numbers.

For web sites, give a brief description of the topic and list the address. For example:

> (4) The replication cycle of HIV: www-micro.msb.le.ac.uk//335/335Replication.html

Course Lecture Schedule

Date:	Lecture Topic:
Jan. 12th:	Introduction
Jan. 14th:	Biological Principles; Evolution
Jan. 16th:	Molecular Evolution; Origin of Cells
Jan. 19th:	**No class - MLK day**
Jan. 21st:	Replication & Gene Expression
Jan. 23rd:	Replication & Gene Expression
Jan. 26th:	Viruses
Jan. 28th:	HIV and AIDS
Jan. 30th:	DISCUSSION: Infectious Disease
Feb. 2nd:	Procaryotes (E. coli)
Feb. 4th:	**Review**
Feb. 6th:	**Exam I**
Feb. 9th:	Eukaryotes: Cell Cycle and Organelles
Feb. 11th:	Chromosomes and Mitosis & Meiosis
Feb. 16th:	Protists (Chlamydomonas)/Sex
Feb. 18th:	Fungi (Neurospora)/Multicellularity
Feb. 20th:	Plants (Zea mays)
Feb. 23rd:	Animals - Invertebrates (Drosophila)
Feb. 25th:	Animals - Vertebrates
Mar. 2nd:	**Review**
Mar. 4th:	**Exam II**
Mar. 7th-15th:	**Spring Break**
Mar. 16th:	Genetic Engineering
Mar. 18th:	Mendelian Genetics
Mar. 23rd:	Human Genetics
Mar. 25th:	Colorblindness
Mar. 27th:	DISCUSSION 2: Genetic Technology: Uses and Abuses
Mar. 30th:	Death & Disease
Apr. 1st:	Cancer
Apr. 3rd:	DISCUSSION 3: Reproductive Rights and Right to Die: Abortion, In Vitro Fertilization and Euthanasia
Apr. 6th:	Animal and Human Behavior
Apr. 8th:	Population Dynamics
Apr. 10th:	**No Class - Good Friday**
Apr. 13th:	**Review**
Apr. 15th:	**Exam III**
Apr. 20th:	Ecosystems
Apr. 22nd:	Human Impact
Apr. 24th:	DISCUSSION 4: Environmental Issues
Apr. 27th:	Biology in the 21st Century
Apr. 29th:	**Final Review**
May 1st:	**Q & A (optional)**
May 8th:	**FINAL EXAM @ 11:30 am - 2:30 pm**

An Environmental Science Approach to Service-Learning in Biology

by Jeffrey A. Simmons

Whenever possible I try to incorporate a service-learning element into the courses that I teach at West Virginia Wesleyan College because it enhances student learning. I have found environmental science courses to be the most amenable to service-learning projects. It is more difficult to come up with projects that are relevant and useful to our small-town community in classes such as Introductory Biology or Human Biology.

Environmental science is full of opportunities for service-learning. The subject matter is more relevant to the local community than that of other biology courses because it includes topics such as economics, health, food, water, individuals' rights, poverty, land, and pollution. Every person deals with at least some of these issues. For example, the unit on energy in my class suggests numerous potential projects: conducting household energy audits, publishing flyers on the most cost-efficient insulation and heating systems, campus energy audits, measuring hot water use, estimating greenhouse gas emissions, raising awareness of alternative energy sources, and building solar cookers.

Furthermore, most people have some level of concern for the environment. It is a prominent topic in news and media reports. People are familiar with (if not exactly knowledgeable about) environmental terms such as greenhouse effect, renewable resources, efficiency, waste, and conservation. Many environmental issues have economic implications, and some of the more controversial issues revolve around personal rights and rights of landownership, making them very personal issues.

Benefits of Service-Learning

In my experience, service-learning enhances the learning experience of students in many ways, most of which are related to motivation. Many pedagogical texts assert that motivation is an essential component of effective student learning. After all, learning takes effort, so a student needs some justification for making that effort. We hope they will be motivated by a desire to excel and to gain knowledge and not by grade acquisition or by fear of punitive measures. In any event, if an instructor can enhance student motivation, students will perform more successfully in class. This has implications for retention at the program, department, and college levels.

Service-learning enhances motivation in several ways: (1) It makes topics relevant to students by involving them in an issue; (2) it helps them gain a sense of ownership of a project or issue; (3) it satisfies the urge many students have to do something tangible and positive for the environment; (4) it gives them an opportunity to gain the satisfaction of performing community service; and (5) it demonstrates that knowledge is useful. I will discuss each of these benefits in turn.

Relevance of Environmental Issues

One gregarious student on our campus related one of her more embarrassing moments. She was studying organic chemistry with several friends in a classroom. Tired and frustrated, she launched into a tirade: "Why do I need to know the structure of benzene?! When will I ever use this? Who cares?" Her friends fell silent and some were snickering. It was then she realized that her chemistry professor was standing in the doorway! Perhaps the most striking aspect of this story is that she was in our honors program — the group of students who tend to be the brightest, most open-minded, and best able to see the larger picture. The professor was eventually able to convince her of the value and utility of the assignment, but it is likely that all students ask themselves similar questions at some point in their college careers. It is, moreover, very easy for students to get so engrossed in grades, assignments, and deadlines that they fail to see the bigger picture. They lose sight of the goals of a liberal arts education.

Service-learning projects automatically make even the most esoteric subject matter relevant to students by involving them in practical applications of the subject. By definition, a service-learning project benefits someone in the community, and the students see firsthand what that benefit is, such as learning about energy efficiency so one can save money each month on one's fuel bill. Students will not cry out, "Why do I need to know this?"

Ownership

Students often come to rely on the professor for everything: reminders of assignments, topics for papers, hints for an answer, etc. We cater to that by using cookbook labs that are easy to prepare and grade. Students report to lab, follow the instructions, and leave. They feel no sense of responsibility, and their creative ability is not encouraged; in fact, in many cases deviation from the "accepted" or "best" answer is punished.

In a service-learning project that involves group implementation of a project, students invest a lot more of themselves and often more time and energy. They are required to be creative as they plan the details of their work. Thus, each project is a little different, and students seem very proud of the creative components they have contributed. While researching the greenhouse effect, one student had read that the Earth's atmosphere is proportionally thinner than the skin of an apple. He was very pleased with himself when he told me about his idea to bring an apple to class and cut it open to show his peers. I think he felt good because he had made a contribution to the group and infused a part of himself into the project. Students also discover that they are responsible for finding supplies and getting things done on time, without reliance on a professor.

Positive Action

Many college students yearn to do something positive for society. Most of the students who enroll in environmental science are concerned about the environment and want to emulate the heroes they have heard about who have cleaned up dump sites, saved a wetland, or stopped development. They would like to accomplish something positive but do not know how or where to begin. Thus, when given an opportunity to help "save the environment," they are happy to participate.

Satisfaction From Community Service

For those students who have never been involved in community service, their first service project can be a real learning experience. They discover the satisfaction and joy of helping others in the community. A survey of my classes showed that about 10 percent of my students had never participated in community service prior to their class with me. The same survey also showed that every one of the students who had had no prior experience indicated that he or she was interested in doing community service. Many of my students tell me that participating in a project that benefits the community makes them feel good. Community service is very popular at West Virginia Wesleyan College, so this percentage of nonparticipants will likely be higher at other institutions.

Knowledge Has a Purpose

The final important lesson that students take home from service projects is that the knowledge they acquire in an environmental science class, and in college in general, is useful. In their service-learning projects, they are asked to apply the knowledge and skills they have learned to a real-life problem. Often *they* become the experts. The community people with whom they interact rely on them for answers. This humbles many students and triggers a rededication to learning, not because the exam is next week but because the knowledge they gain is valuable.

Examples of Service-Learning Projects

Below are some service-learning projects with which I have had success. They may or may not be appropriate at every school, depending on class size, equipment and facilities available, and time. However, I would like to dispel the notion that service-learning projects are feasible only in small or upper-level classes. I regularly include them in a nonmajors' environmental science course that typically enrolls 50 to 75 students.

Well Water Testing

One of the first service-learning projects I attempted grew out of a potential research question I was investigating. West Virginia has a large rural population living at or below the poverty level. Many industrial activities (e.g., coal mining and forestry) used to be located in these rural communities. Did poor rural families suffer indirect health threats from these activities? I wanted to determine the quality of the drinking water of a wide range of rural households. So I replaced the traditional municipal water testing laboratory exercise in my environmental science class with the project Well Water Testing. Knowing that they were part of an original pilot study and that they were aiding rural families by providing free water tests, students immediately became excited about the project. The difficult part was collecting the samples. We placed an ad in the local newspaper and asked a rural church to participate in the study. Most residents were happy to have their water tested. Using basic equipment, students conducted a chemical analysis of the samples. A few earned extra credit by entering the data into a computer and producing reports that were then mailed back to the households.

Visit to Elementary School

Sending college students to a local elementary school to teach a lesson or two can be done in any discipline, not just environmental science. The students in my course are required to create an original lesson in environmental science for a designated primary school class. I give them one laboratory period to plan and coordinate the lesson. Typically, the students have to spend some time studying an environmental issue before they present it. Even though they do not learn much new material in a lab like this, they do learn that environmental science is relevant and that we are responsible for passing our knowledge on to the next generation. Furthermore, this exercise reinforces their understanding of the lab material.

In addition, the elementary school teachers benefit by getting a short respite when the college students visit. The students make the children feel special and important, and the children now look forward to our Earth Day visit. They have developed a very positive outlook on environmental science.

Household Energy Audit

One of our college offices recently moved into a house just off campus. Like most of the houses in that part of town, this building was built early in the 20th century. I adapted one of our standard labs on household energy so that students would actually conduct an energy audit on this house and make recommendations to the college about how to decrease heating costs. During lab time we all walked over to the house, inspected it from top to bottom, and took measurements. Back in the lab we estimated the amount of heat lost through walls (uninsulated), windows (single pane), and the ceiling. Then we estimated how much money would be saved by insulating the walls and/or ceiling, replacing the windows, or replacing the furnace. These recommendations were passed on the administration. Students learned some very practical skills (how to read an electric meter, what type of insulation is best) and were able to apply what they had learned in class to a real-life situation.

Independent Study/Research Projects

Because independent projects go into greater depth than lecture topics, and because they are not limited by curricular requirements, they provide an excellent vehicle for studying real-world problems. Students can be asked to assess regional air quality or the level of pollution in a local waterway. They can measure regional ambient noise levels or compare the types of indicator organisms found in two streams. The knowledge thus gained will be valuable to the community, while the students are exhilarated by working on an original problem of concern to real people.

Summary

If nothing else, I hope I have demonstrated the tremendous potential of service-learning in environmental science courses. For someone who has never tried a service-learning project, experimenting in an environmental science course would be a great way to get started. Indeed, I find it a rewarding experience in and of itself as well as a motivational tool for my classes. It benefits me, the students, and the community.

College/community relations are strengthened and improved when a college directs some of its impressive resources and energy to the community. In this way, the college becomes a contributing member of the community instead of just an isolated institution. Every community has needs and can benefit from a college's outreach activities. Every college has students who can benefit from real-world experience. It only makes sense that we match these two needs.

OUACHITA TECHNICAL COLLEGE

Acknowledgments

My first attempt at service-learning (a visit to French Creek Elementary School) was accomplished with funding from the Corporation for National Service and Campus Compact during the spring 1996 semester.

Service-Learning in Botany:
A Public School Project

by Nancy K. Prentiss

Helping to create community is one of the benefits of service-learning. Service-learning projects provide college students with the chance to experience and learn that community service is multifaceted, and that no matter what a person's area of interest or skill level, everyone has something to offer the community at large.

While there are many apparent applications for service-learning in the fields of education and the social sciences, science instructors do not always see comparable ways for incorporating service-learning into natural science courses. Traditional science courses involve learning a hefty assemblage of concepts that do not seem immediately applicable to the everyday life of a local community. Furthermore, college students are rarely provided with enough experiences to use their newly developed knowledge and skills in the real world.

And yet, as scientists, we have an obligation to engage the general public in our respective fields so that future generations can better understand science and environmental issues. The challenge put forth to science instructors is to find community service projects that address goals meaningful to all participants.

Environmental studies are now included in most public schools. However, topics are often isolated within a generalized science curriculum. While most children have had at least some minimal exposure to natural settings, the emphasis is often on experiencing a whole system, such as a pond or forest, rather than on looking in more detail at the parts that make up the whole.

Nationally, the public school system has suffered critical budget cuts in recent years, leaving little or no funding to provide "extras" either for the curriculum or for teacher development. This has occurred at a time when environmental studies should be at the forefront, as one of the basics of a solid education. Schools in rural America have ready access to the natural history of an area, and even urban schools can usually find some natural habitat within the confines of the city. However, these valuable resources largely go unnoticed and unused by the majority of public school teachers, who lack the foundation to teach the basics of natural history and conservation.

Under ever-encroaching pressures by society to develop wilderness areas and exploit resources, it is critical that young citizens have a good knowledge base in conservation issues so they can understand what components of the environment might be lost through development. An introductory study of native flora provides a good introduction to natural communities, which are normally first described by the vegetation growing within them. Such study may serve as a base for later environmental studies.

What follows is a description of a service-learning project that has been incorporated into the Field Botany course at the University of Maine at Farmington (UMF) (see the abbreviated version of my syllabus reproduced at the end of this chapter). This project challenges college students to solidify their knowledge base of native Maine flora by teaching the basics of wildflower identification to teachers and students in local public schools.

The Project

The idea for this project began several years ago when three students in my Field Botany class opted to conduct service-learning projects at three different schools in lieu of writing a traditional term paper. UMF students designed lesson plans and met with teachers to define their project objectives. The UMF students then taught lessons on wildflower and fern identification and conservation.

The teachers hosting the service-learning projects in botany unanimously indicated that they wanted to be included in future service-learning projects. When asked to evaluate whether the service-learning project would prompt further activities of this nature, one teacher responded, "Yes, most definitely. I would like to plan my own activities following this style." The statements that follow were taken from self-evaluations by the UMF students who conducted the service-learning projects that year.

I am convinced that this type of alternate education accomplishes much more (for elementary students) than sitting in the classroom looking at books all the time.

I found this experience very valuable to me as a future teacher. I have already spoken with the teachers involved about doing a follow-up in the fall. I feel that for nonscience majors such as myself, service projects are a better way to learn the materials covered than [would be] a more traditional research paper.

These initial projects served as a pilot study of the feasibility of teaching concepts of wildflower identification to elementary students, and the readiness of elementary students to grasp the material using sophisticated field guides.

In spring 1997, I incorporated a more extensive service-learning project as part of my May term course, Field Botany. The project was supported in part by a $2,000 Maine Campus Compact grant, which was funded by the federal Corporation for National and Community Service's Learn and Serve America: Higher Education program. The goals of the project were threefold:

1. To expand the service-learning component of the Field Botany course so that approximately 14 UMF students could incorporate what they learned into teaching wildflower and fern identification to 50 fourth and fifth graders in the local public Cascade Brook School (CBS), in Farmington, Maine. UMF students would also help the fourth and fifth graders design and implement a nature trail in the woods surrounding their school.

2. To provide enrichment for public school students in the area of natural history — specifically, native wildflowers and ferns of the region.

3. To help local elementary school teachers expand their knowledge base in the natural sciences and environmental studies, to assist them with some long-term outdoor classroom studies, and to add greater interest and depth to their science units through hands-on learning.

Project Design

Project planning was critical to the initiative's success. Here I emphasize that it is important that both parties form a partnership rather than a presenter-recipient arrangement. Also, for a project to meet with ultimate success, one should iron out all the fine details regarding everyone's expectations. Prior to the commencement of the course, I identified three students who wanted to help with the planning of the project. These students happened to be education majors with a science concentration. We met four times with the two public school teachers involved, outlining the logistics of meshing the busy schedules of all participants.

Our initial discussion included five major topics:

• *Classroom instruction and design:* How will it work? Should miniworkshops be held inside and outside? What are the elementary students capable of? How structured should workshops be? How much background information do teachers/students need ahead of time? What materials are needed for teachers? How much class time do teachers want to devote to this topic?

• *Scheduling:* What other conflicting events are occurring during the time period? What does the calendar outline look like for the project?

• *Nature trail and herbarium:* What do teachers have in mind for overall size of the nature trail? What materials are desired for signs? Do teachers see this as a useful, ongoing project? Will the herbarium be protected and incorporated into the school library? How can UMF help the public school further the establishment of a more permanent outdoor classroom?

• *Evaluation:* What do teachers want students to get out of it? How do teachers want to assess learning in fourth- and fifth-grade students?

• *Involving others:* Can we include parent volunteers for extra hands-on help? How can we ensure that the project can continue (that the trail would be maintained, etc.)? Does the project have the potential to draw others in to keep it going?

Implementation

We established three dates for the two parties (UMF students and public school students) to meet as a single group in a workshop session, and then identified time periods that would remain open for individual UMF students to work independently with small groups (four to a group) of public school students.

UMF students worked cooperatively with one another and with the teachers to plan the teaching units, dividing the course material into smaller subunits to teach the basics of plant identification. During subsequent sessions (minimum of three sessions required), UMF students taught CBS students and their teachers how to key out and recognize some common spring wildflowers and ferns in the woods on the school property. They also helped the public school students make a master list of plants encountered in the woods surrounding the school. Public school students learned how to preserve and catalog plants for a school herbarium, and learned which flowers not to pick.

At the end of the project, all participants took a field trip to a National Audubon Society sanctuary, which presented students with a different habitat as well as a professional nature trail. UMF students, who were given a detailed instruction sheet (reproduced at the end of this chapter), were asked to adhere to public school rules and coordinate information among themselves with regard to the trail.

Materials and Resources

Teaching plant identification requires appropriate field guides (books) and tools. Experience with both children and adult learners indicates that if they have ready access to books and magnifiers, they are more active students and participants. The books purchased with grant funds were lent on a temporary basis, and then recycled for use in future workshops. Hand-held lenses (10X) — necessary tools for plant identification and appreciation of floral structure and fern characteristics — were also lent. In addition, students shared plant presses, herbarium paper, and labels to collect, preserve, and identify herbarium specimens for an herbarium to be established at Cascade Brook School. Later in the semester, still other materials were donated by local hardware stores and lumberyards.

The day-long field trip to the National Audubon Society sanctuary allowed students to experience a professional nature trail (three miles), and gave them an opportunity to encounter a mature, climaxed forest with its emerging spring wildflowers. Spring offers some of the most exciting wildflowers of the year, and it is a good time to hook students on plant study, since the variety of plants in the spring is not so plentiful as to be overwhelming. At the sanctuary, students could see firsthand the workings of the Audubon Society, which has the goal of "long-term protection and wise use of our natural resources."

Reflection

Following the workshops, and during their regular class time, UMF students reflected on how the service-learning project influenced their own learning of the course material. They also kept a written account of the project as a part of their field journal. Follow-up presentations on the project were provided by several participating students throughout the following school year. A summary of reflective activities would include the following:

1. Students were asked to document whether their involvement in the project enhanced their learning of the course material. At the end of the course, each UMF student turned in a written evaluation of both the general project and his or her individual participation. As part of the regular field journal required for the Field Botany course, each UMF student made entries on his or her participation in the service-learning project. During the class following each workshop, students also reflected as a group on the effectiveness of their presentations and assessed whether they had met their objectives for that day.

2. The fourth- and fifth-grade teachers involved in the project gave written answers to questions provided on a survey form. They evaluated the project with regard to the effectiveness of the UMF students, the level of participation and learning by the fourth and fifth graders, and perceptions of the project's value to the school and community.

3. The fourth- and fifth-grade students filled out survey forms that included questions that asked them what they had learned and about their perceptions of working with UMF students.

Evaluation

UMF Students

The university students, who did regular reflection through a daily journal, class debriefings, and a final reflection report, unanimously agreed that they had learned the material and skills more thoroughly as a direct result of this project. At first, not all embraced the idea of working with young children as a course requirement. However, there was 100-percent cooperation. In the end, all realized that a great deal of bonding (and learning) had occurred. Each student said he or she thought the project was worthwhile and that he or she would choose to do it again.

Furthermore, every UMF student communicated to me in some way a desire for other, similar experiences. One student planned to construct a nature trail at the retirement center in his home community on the Maine coast. Several students asked me to keep them informed if there were any related projects the following summer they could be a part of. Three students planned follow-up work on the CBS nature trail. One student felt this work would help him get the summer employment he wanted. Another student said the experience had prompted her to switch her major to biology, even though she previously had not liked the subject.

Comments from UMF students regarding the service-learning experience included the following:

Going out and using and sharing what I have learned made me feel like I was a part of something bigger than a typical class. While it is rewarding to have the knowledge for yourself, I think that when that knowledge is shared and used in a positive way it gives you an even better feeling about what you know and have done with it — it has for me.

If I had the choice and the options, all of the courses I take would involve some type of [service] work, especially if it involves hands-on learning such as the nature trail project. My experiences from working with the students and this class have led me to think about projects that I could be involved in or involve others in.

So I wasn't learning just for myself, I was learning it for other people so that I may pass on the skills and pleasure that go along with keying out the native flora and learning about the environment we live in.

Some days went better than others, but overall we learned a lot together, cooperated, and were respectful to one another. They were pleased with their accomplishments, and so was I of them!

Public School Teachers

Public school teachers were very positive about the project. They asked us to continue it the next year despite the fact that there would be a turnover in college students. They also felt the project augmented the public school goal of increasing cooperative learning and student bonding across all grades. It encouraged fourth and fifth graders to work together toward a common goal.

Comments from CBS teachers regarding the service-learning experience included:

I know that it's generated a new interest to continue trail work at the school. This has been the most worthwhile project to take place on our trail system since it began six years ago.

I liked the way we as teachers were involved in the planning stages.

I am very receptive of this project. It came at a great time of year when the kids needed a different learning atmosphere other than just in the classroom. I was amazed at how fast they learned information.

The fifth graders were very receptive to the UMF students. It was interesting to watch the interaction of the two groups.

Fourth- and Fifth-Grade Students

Fourth- and fifth-grade students experienced immediate success in learning the basics of wildflower identification. They also learned to recognize many common plants at sight. They started a plant collection (herbarium), with at least 50 plants pressed, mounted, and labeled for the school library herbarium.

They also assisted in making an attractive trail guide for the self-guided nature trail, putting out the permanent wooden signs and finishing off the trail. They noticed that many of the flowers had disappeared and that new ones were coming out. Many expressed a desire to continue with the trails, and some wanted to continue in the fall with a nature club. Many stated that their nature trail was better than the one they had visited at the Audubon Society sanctuary.

On the basis of entries in student log books and follow-up student evaluations, we can assert that the fourth and fifth graders developed a heightened interest and awareness of the native flora in the environment. Comments from CBS students regarding the service-learning experience included:

I can teach others the names and how to identify flowers.

I used to tramp through the woods not caring. Now I care!

The project has changed me so now I watch where I step.

Now I go out looking for flowers.

Other Findings

Having taught this course three times, I have been able to make useful observations on the assimilation of knowledge and skills by the college students. While the sample size has not been large enough to conduct any statistical studies, there is strong evidence that through their service-learning projects students learned the course material better than in previous years. They consistently did better on all tests given, and appeared to take a sincere interest in the success of the nature trail project and their charges. Coincidentally, about half of the UMF students in the course were education majors, and they eagerly embraced this project as a way to gain more practical, hands-on experience. The project benefited directly from their enthusiasm for and previous experience in working with young students.

Relationships formed between UMF students and CBS students. An exchange of addresses and a sharing of photos also took place. UMF students had extra photos made for the young students in their groups. At each trail outing, CBS students quickly migrated to their leaders.

Good learning can take place outside the confines of the traditional classroom. UMF students and CBS teachers were able to see firsthand how different children learn differently. Awareness of nature has recently been recognized as one of the eight "multiple intelligences" recognized by Howard Gardner. One fifth-grade boy, who has never been "academic" in school, just lost himself in this project. His mother offered the following unsolicited comment: "This [nature trail work] is all Matt has talked about since you started this project. He has never said one thing about school all year until now. He hasn't stopped talking about it."

Summary and Further Application

There appears to be plenty of room to extend this project in the public schools and to conduct similar service-learning projects throughout the area. Since the project first began, several local public school teachers have asked to be considered for inclusion in future projects. The existing nature trail at the Cascade Brook School is also being used to garner support from an area paper company to build an outdoor classroom at the school. Some university students have expressed an interest in advising a fledgling nature club formed as a direct offshoot of this project.

CBS teachers indicate they now feel more confident in teaching the unit without intensive direction. However, they have asked to have more UMF students back during subsequent years to build on the learning experience for students and teachers alike.

Field Botany (BIO 167) - May Term 1997

Instructor: Nancy Prentiss

Office: Ricker 27 (second floor)
Voice Mail 778-7396 (Leave message anytime - I will check twice daily for messages)
E-mail: Prentiss@maine.maine.edu
Call me if you can't attend class!!!

Meeting: 11 Preble Hall and "in the field"

Time: Tuesday and Wednesday afternoons from 1:00 to 3:30 p.m.*
Thursdays from 9:30 a.m. to 3:30 p.m.*

*Note: If class participants agree, the hours of some field trips may be extended to allow for travel time in addition, an all day field trip is planned for Friday, June 6.

MOST CLASS MEETINGS WILL INVOLVE FIELD TRIPS AND WE WILL LEAVE <u>PROMPTLY</u> AT THE BEGINNING OF EACH CLASS. PLEASE LEAVE A MESSAGE IF YOU WILL BE ABSENT SO WE DON'T WASTE TIME WAITING FOR YOU!!! PLAN TO ARRIVE AT THE CLASSROOM AT LEAST FIVE MINUTES <u>PRIOR</u> TO STARTING TIME. YOUR GRADE WILL BE COMPROMISED IF YOU MISS CLASS, PLEASE BE RESPONSIBLE!!!!!!!!!

Texts:

1. *Newcomb's Wildflower Guide*, by Lawrence Newcomb 1977
2. *Ferns of Northeastern United States*, by Farida A. Wiley 1973
3. *The North Woods*, by Peter Marchand 1987

References:

1. *Kate Furbish and the Flora of Maine*, by Ada and Frank Graham, Jr. 1995
2. *Natural Landscapes of Maine: as a Classification of Ecosystems and Natural Communities*, by Maine Natural Areas Program.
3. *Bogs of the Northeast*, by Charles Johnson 1985

Additional Requirements:

1. 10X pocket magnifier (Available in the bookstore)
2. Herbarium mounting paper (Available in the bookstore) for those doing herbariums

Other:

1. Plant Press (Provided for you - must be returned with plant collection)
2. Herbarium Labels (Provided for you)
3. A pocket knife is handy for fern identification

Goals:

To further an appreciation for the natural history of our world, while concentrating on plant communities in selected Maine habitats. The purpose is not to learn all the plants available to us, but rather, to learn how to identify them and to recognize some basic plant communities. A second goal is to teach and guide others in the concepts of wildflower identification and conservation.

Format:

We will take field trips during each meeting time to maximize opportunities to see plants in their natural habitats. Expect to go outside, even if it is raining. (Plan to get wet and dirty.) This course falls well within the peak of the black fly season, so dress accordingly, and bring bug repellent, hat, bandanna, etc. Also wear some sturdy boots or old sneakers and plan to get into the "muck." You'll also want a snack, bag lunch and lots of water for Thursday field trips. We sometimes get wet on canoe trips - you may want to bring a Change of clothes and shoes! Field trips are subject to change, depending on the weather, plant emergence and accessibility. Suggestions for alternative study sites are welcome. New This Year: A significant portion of this course includes UMF students committing out-of-class time to work with students at the local elementary school (Cascade Brook School) on their nature trail project.

Course Requirements:

A total of 400 points for this 3-credit course will be allocated as follows:

I.   **HERBARIUM COLLECTION:**   (200 points)

A traditional herbarium collection will be made by preserving, mounting, and identifying 50 **NATIVE** species of plants. Details for preparation will be discussed in class. Other options, such as drawings or photographs will be considered as a substitute for the plant herbarium (Ask me 1st) The collections will include fifty specimens from the following categories:

A. Herbaceous or woody wildflowers. (30 to 50 species)

(NO THREATENED OR ENDANGERED SPECIES, OR ELSE!   50 PTS. DEDUCTED!

-- If you aren't sure if a plant is threatened or not, **DON'T** pick it! (Check the list)

-- Include only native species from at least 20 different families.

-- No cultivated or introduced species (aliens) allowed.

-- You may use native shrubs, such as a Common Eldeberry, or Shadbush.

B. Ferns. (Up to 20 native, non-endangered species):

II.   **QUIZZES:** (60 points)
1. Terminology for identification of flowering plants (10 points)
2. Terminology for fern identification (10 points)
3. Identification of "mystery plants" (40 points)

III.   **SERVICE- LEARNING PROJECT:** (100 points)
The service-learning component this year replaces the "typical term paper." We will work with 4th and 5th graders at Cascade Brook School (CBS) in Farmington, to teach them skills in wildflower and fern identification, and then to help them implement a nature trail, which will be accessible to the greater Farmington community. Your own learning should enhanced through the teaching of your new skills to others.

This project is being funded by a federal grant awarded by "*Learn and Serve America - Corporation for Service-Learning.*"

You are expected to participate fully in class workshops, as well as to make commitments on your own time to meet with small groups of CBS students to help them with their designated portion of the nature trail. Finally, you are expected to evaluate your own participation in the service-learning project. Evaluation of your effort will be as follows:

1. My evaluation of your participation with CBS students and in-class (UMF) reflection. (20%)

2. Your self evaluation through your journal and follow-up report. (60%)

3. CBS teacher evaluation of your effectiveness in helping CBS students meet their goals. (20%)

IV.   **JOURNAL** (40 points)
A journal/notebook will be kept during all class field trips and your own explores. Include class field notes, work with CBS students, sketches, descriptions of plants, habitats, micro-habitats, family characteristics, plant associations within communities, variations within species, seasonal progression, attitudinal changes, dates and locations of specimen collections, poems, etc. It should be a detailed as possible and although your journal will not be graded for artistry, you should feel free to be creative.

Instructions

School "Etiquette":
Arrive 5 minutes before you are scheduled.
Check in at the front office and sign the volunteer log.
Introduce yourself to the teacher.
Respect the rights and routines of teachers and students.
Inform the teacher or call the school if you won't be there.

Trail Work:
Take field guide, notebook, markers, flagging tape and stakes with you.
Remind students to bring notebooks, guides, plant press and magnifiers.
Keep a running list of all plants identified.
Try to be selective on what you identify -- (there is no need to ID every trout lily.)
Get the students back in time for their next activity.

Coordination:
Turn in your plant list to the "list organizer" who will coordinate as master list of plants.
Pin point as best you can on the map any "unusual" or less common plants.
Let me know if your schedule changes.

Other:
Feel free to visit the trail alone to get to know plants better and spend more time identifying them.
Ask for help when you need it.
Be assertive -- be in charge of your group. If they are running ahead, set some rules and boundaries.
You are required to meet with your group at least 3 times -- feel free to do more!

Reflection:
After each experience with your group, please write down your impressions. How is the project progressing from your perspective. What suggestions might you make for yourself or for others for future meetings. Does you work with the CBS students influence how and to what extent you learn the material? If so, how? Would you be learning the material quickly if you were not involved with this project? Please be as detailed possible. What worked well? What didn't work so well?

Service-learning Information:
You may be interested in knowing that this project is being funded by a grant awarded by the Maine Campus Compact. The grant monies are provided by the Federal Corporation for National and Community Service, Learn and Serve America, Higher Education Program. UMF is a member of Maine Campus Compact, a group of universities and colleges throughout Maine that is committed to Service-learning.

Service Stimulates Science Learning in At-Risk Kids: The Millikin Model

by Marianne Robertson

Millikin University is at the forefront of the current drive toward service-learning in Illinois. Indeed, the service-learning experience is essential to Millikin's mission of helping students develop a well-rounded approach to problem solving. My own service-learning project also seeks to expose elementary school students to a university environment with the hope that they will themselves pursue postsecondary education.

I specifically chose to link the Millikin biology program to Washington Elementary School because Washington Elementary has a low budget and few resources, and is located in a depressed, inner-city neighborhood. The majority of its students are on the free lunch program and are being raised by single parents or relatives, or are in foster care. Millikin students work with sixth graders from the school through my spring semester course Animal Behavior — an upper-level biology course offered to juniors and seniors (my syllabus is reproduced at the end of this chapter). Each student in the course serves as a science mentor to three sixth graders, and assists them in conducting research projects in the area of animal behavior.

The university's Animal Behavior laboratory is designed so that students can choose an area of interest (courtship behavior, predation, communication, defense mechanisms, mimicry, etc.) during the first month of the semester and conduct a rigorous research project during the remainder of the semester. I require all students to give an oral presentation, write a research paper, and participate in an undergraduate research symposium at the end of the semester. Such independent research teaches students how to *apply* the scientific method and helps them to appreciate the unexpected problems and stresses associated with doing original research. Furthermore, students are better able to assist others in a research project if they must go through the same process themselves, though at an advanced level. This arrangement allows Millikin students both to conduct college-level research *and* to teach what they have learned to others by assisting young learners with a separate research project designed by them with assistance from their Millikin mentors.

Once the Animal Behavior students have begun their own research project, they and I meet with the principal and a parent-teacher liaison from Washington Elementary. This allows the elementary school personnel to meet my students and get an idea of their personalities and interests before finalizing decisions as to which sixth graders will be involved in the program. School administrators, in collaboration with the sixth-grade teachers, choose the youngsters they feel will benefit most from this individualized attention. The opportunity to participate in the animal behavior program serves as an incentive to the sixth graders to strive for good grades and attitudes. By mid-February, each Animal Behavior student is assigned three sixth graders to work with until mid-April. In this way, at-risk youngsters get a chance to be involved in hands-on scientific activity with a university student prior to their entering high school.

The elementary school students come to the university weekly to work on their projects with Millikin students. These projects have focused on a variety of topics, such as tarantula locomotion, the effect of water temperatures on activity in Japanese fire-belly newts, learning in dwarf Siberian hamsters, color change in green anoles and green tree frogs, and aggressive behavior in Siamese fighting fish. The semester culminates with a science fair at the elementary school. Washington students present their work in their school science lab to an audience of parents, teachers, and the principal as well as Millikin faculty, staff, administrators, and students. In addition, the school hosts a parent-student night to display student work.

This project has a positive impact on both the community and the Millikin students. The latter have their learning constantly reinforced by being required to teach concepts to others. They also learn the value of planning ahead and budgeting their time. They learn quickly that sixth graders need structure, guidance, and constant encouragement. Initially, some of the students may view the course's service-learning component as merely "one more requirement." However, service-learning is something an individual has to *experience* to realize its impact. Without exception, students get more deeply involved in the project than they expect to, working many more hours than are required.

In short, the service-learning component adds a whole new dimension to class dynamics. Teamwork and collaboration seem to arise naturally from it, and it provides a better means of assessing student learning than exams alone would. Seeing students teach and use what they have learned in class gives me a far more accurate assessment of their performance than would mere memorization and regurgitation of material. To take lecture material and make it accessible to sixth graders requires an understanding on the part of the Millikin students that goes far beyond reading the pages of a book.

In addition to such on-site assessment, I require all students to keep a journal throughout the semester. Here they are challenged to make connections between their own independent research projects and the projects they are guiding the sixth graders through. They also record all assignments they give their students, and assess each student's work weekly. The sixth-grade teachers and I then read all student journals and discuss the progress of all students, Millikin and Washington. Finally, the Washington school parent-teacher liaison and a service-learning colleague from Illinois Campus Compact lead the university students through reflective sessions. The students consistently indicate that they learn much more by having a service-learning component in the course, and have been very successful in making important connections between community and classroom.

What perhaps impresses me most about incorporation of a service-learning project is the way in which it helps students who tend to be quiet in class really come out of their shells. I cannot describe how rewarding it is to listen to the students teach each other! I see my students exhibiting patience, understanding, emotion, scholarship, and a love of biology that would not surface in a traditional classroom. Indeed, I have never seen my students as enthusiastic and self-confident as they are after completing their work at Washington Elementary. To say they feel fulfilled is an understatement.

But the project also makes a difference in the lives of the participating elementary school children. The sixth graders change dramatically during the course of the semester. They become less interested in responding to peer pressure and begin expressing independent thoughts and ideas. They also change from an initial attitude of indifference to one of overt enthusiasm and love of doing science. As I mentioned above, many of these children come from economically disadvantaged households and receive little academic encouragement in their home environment. However, during the course of the project, it is not unusual to hear them begin talking about what they will do when *they* enter college!

Incorporating service-learning into my course Animal Behavior has fostered self-confidence, critical thinking, teamwork, and an appreciation for science in all the students involved — Millikin and Washington. The university students better appreciate the privilege of a college education and become better scientists with a stronger grasp on the course material. The sixth graders realize that dreams can come true, that there are people who care about their education, and that hard work and dedication can open doors to people at all economic levels. Finally, I feel I myself learn as much as anyone, and develop an especially strong relationship with my students through this kind of interaction. For me, service-learning adds an extra joy to the rewards of teaching and never ceases to further my own education.

Acknowledgments

Funds for this program were made possible through a series of grants from the Corporation for National Service and the national office of Campus Compact.

ANIMAL BEHAVIOR

Instructor: Dr. Marianne Robertson
Office: S217B
Office Phone: 24-3754
Office Hours: 8:00-9:30 MWF

Texts:

Animal Behavior, Alcock, 5th ed., 1989
The Trials of Life, Attenborough, 1990 (Optional)

Course Objectives:

1. To develop an understanding of the fundamental principles of animal behavior
2. To develop a comparative evolutionary appreciation of animal behavior
3. To interpret current literature on animal behavior
4. To participate in **Service Learning** and **APPLY** your knowledge to assist others
5. To gain insight into methods of behavioral research
6. Laboratories emphasize observation, description, and formulation of questions and testable hypotheses and **APPLICATION** of the scientific method in a rigorous manner

Class Participation:

This semester, I have scheduled class discussions following most chapters. These discussions will be on current papers that reinforce the material presented in Alcock and show you the **APPLICATION** of what you are learning. As upper level students, you are each expected to actively **PARTICIPATE** in class discussions. I expect you to read the assignments from Alcock, as well as the journal articles, BEFORE you come to lecture. I will hit the high points, but I will not repeat the text!! You should come to class prepared to **THINK, DISCUSS, INTERACT** and LEARN! Please CHALLENGE yourselves and me!!

Attendance Policy:

Students are expected to attend and PARTICIPATE in all lectures and laboratories. Attendance and participation are considered when assigning grades. Lack of participation can raise OR lower your grade. The student is responsible for all material and for all announcements presented in class and lab whether he/she is present or not. Makeup exams will only be allowed for well verified, excused absences and must be made up on the 1st day the student returns to class. Laboratory assignments must be TYPED, and one letter grade per day is deducted for late papers. These deductions apply if a report is turned in late on the due date. If you have an unexcused absence the day a report is due, it must be turned in early to avoid deductions.

TENTATIVE LECTURE SCHEDULE

DATE   TOPIC

1/15   Introduction; *Tenebrio* Observations

1/17   Ch. 1 An Evolutionary Approach to Animal Behavior
1/20   Class Discussion
            J. Weiner. 1994. The Beak of the Finch
                Ch. 4 - Darwin's Beaks
                Ch. 5 - A Special Providence
                Ch. 7 - 25,000 Darwin's

1/22   Ch. 2 The Diversity of Behavior
1/24   Class Discussion
            Bernays & Chapman. 1994. Host-Plant Selection by Phytophagous Insects.
            Ch. 6 - Effects of Experience, pp. 206-229
            Richard Dawkins. 1989. The Selfish Gene. Ch. 1. Why are People? pp. 1-11

1/27   Ch. 3 The Genetics of Behavior
1/29   Class Discussion
            Bouchard, Lykken, McGue, Segal, & Tellegen. 1990. Sources of Human Psychological Differences: The
                Minnesota Study of Twins Reared Apart. Science, 250.223- 228.
            Richard Dawkins. 1989. The Selfish Gene.
                Ch. 10 - You Scratch My Back, I'll Ride on Yours
1/31   Guest Lecture - Genetics of Sexual Behavior in *Drosophila*, G. Cote

2/3   **Workshop, Katana Schultz, Parent Liaison, Washington Elementary**

2/5   Ch. 6 The Organization of Behavior
2/7   Class Discussion
            Sweeney, B. M. and M. B. Borgese. 1989. A circadian rhyLhm in cell division in a prokaryote, the
                cyanobacterium *Synechococcus* WH7803. J. Psychol., 25:183-186.   JOE
            Sweeney, B. M. 1987. Rhythmic Phenomena in Plants. Ch. 3. Rhythms that match environmental
                periodicities: day and night.
            Seachrist, L. 1994. Sea turtles master migration with magnetic memories. Science, 264:661-662.
2/10   Ch. 7 The Evolution of Behavior: Historical Pathways
            Evening Video (The Burgess Shale) & Dinner @ Robertson Zoo
2/12   Class Discussion
            Gould, Stephen J . 1986. Evolution and the Triumph of Homology, or Why History Matters. Am.
                Scientist, 74:60-69.
            Dawkins, Richard. 1986. The Blind Watchmaker. Ch. 3 - Accumulating Small Change, pp. 43-74

2/14   **EXAM I**

2/17   **Service Learning w/ Washington Elementary**

2/19   Ch. 8 The Evolution of Adaptations
2/21   CLASS DEBATE
            Gould, S. J. and R. C. Lewontin. 1981. The spandrels of San Marco and the Panglossian paradigm: a
                critique of the adaptationist programme. Proceedings of the Royal Society of London B,
                205:581—598.
            Brown, J. L. 1982. The adaptationist program. Science, 217:884-
                886.

Davies, N. B., A. F. G. Bourke, and M. de L. Brooke. 1989. Cuckoos and parasitic ants: interspecific brood parasitism as an evolutionary arms race. Trends in Ecology and Evolution, 4:274—278.

2/24   **Service Learning w/ Washington Elementary**

2/26   Ch. 9 The Evolution of Communication
2/28   <u>Class Discussion</u>
Krebs, J. R. and R. Dawkins. 1984. Animal Signals: Mind-Reading and Manipulation. In: Behavioural Ecology, an Evolutionary Approach, 2nd ed. pp. 380-402.
Holldobler, B. and E. 0. Wilson. 1994. Journey to the Ants, A Story of Scientific Exploration. "How Ants Communicate" pp. 41-58.
Holldobler, B. 1971. Communication between ants and their guests. Scientific American, 224:86-95.

3/3   Ch. 10 Finding a Place to Live
3/5   Service Learning w/ Washington Elementary
3/7   <u>Class Discussion</u>
Holekamp, K. E. and P. W. Sherman. 1989. Why male ground
     squirrels disperse. American Scientist, 77:232-239.
Riechert, S. E. 1986. Spider fights as a test of evolutionary game theory. American Scientist, 74:604—610.

3/10   **Service Learning w/ Washington Elementary**

3/12   Ch. 11 Adaptive Feeding Behavior
3/14   <u>Class Discussion</u>
Zach, R. 1979. Shell dropping: Decision making and optimal foraging in northwestern crows.
     Behaviour, 68:106-117.
Yeargan, K. V. 1988. Ecology of a bolas spider, *Mastophora hutchinsoni*: phenology, hunting tactics, and
     evidence for aggressive chemical mimicry. Oecologia, 74:524-530.

3/17   **Service Learning w/ Washington Elementary**

3/19   Ch. 12 Coping with Predators Adaptively
3/21   <u>Class Discussion</u>
Mather, M. H. and B. D. Roitberg. 1987. A sheep in wolf's clothing: Tephritid flies mimic spider
     predators. Science, 236:308-310.
Heinrich, B. 1979. Foraging strategies of caterpillars: leaf damage and possible predator avoidance
     strategies. Oecologia, 42:325-337.
Caro, T. M. 1986. The functions of stotting: a review of the hypotheses. Animal Behaviour, 34:649-662.

3/24—3/31   **SPRING BREAK**

4/2   **Service Learning w/ Washington Elementary**

4/4   **EXAM II**

4/7   **Complete Service Learning w/ Washington Elementary**

4/9   Ch. 13 Male & Female Reproductive Tactics
READ THESE BEFORE COMING TO CLASS!
Dawkins, R. 1989. The Selfish Gene. Ch. 9. Battle of the Sexes
Thornhill, R. and J. Alcock. 1983. The Evolution of Insect Mating Systems. Ch. 3 - Sexual Selection
     Theory, pp. 51-89.

4/11   **Butler University Undergraduate Research Symposium**

4/14   Ch. 13 Continued

4/16	Ch. 14	The Ecology of Mating Systems
4/18	Ch. 14	Continued

4/21   **Millikin University Poster Symposium**

4/23   Ch. 15 Caring for Offspring
4/25   Ch. 16 The Ecology of Social Behavior
4/28   <u>Class Discussion</u>
        DeVries, P. J. 1992. Singing Caterpillars, Ants and Symbiosis. Scientific American, pp. 76-82.
        Holldobler, B. and E. 0. Wilson. 1994. Journey to the Ants, A Story of Scientific Exploration.
        "The Origin of Cooperation" pp. 95-106.
        "The Superorganism" pp. 107-122.
        "Social Parasites: Breaking the Code" pp. 123-141
        "The Trophobionts" pp. 143-155.

4/30   **EXAM III**

5/2   Ch. 17 An Evolutionary Approach to Animal Behavior
5/5   <u>Class Discussion</u>
        Wilson, E. 0. 1975. Sociobiology. Ch. 26 - Man: From Sociobiology to Sociology. pp. 271-301.

GRADING
LECTURE

3 Exams at 100 points each   300
Participation in Class Discussions   100
Service Learning   150
Cumulative Final Exam   <u>100</u>
            Total Lecture Points   650

LAB SCHEDULE

<u>DATE</u>   <u>TOPIC</u>

1/14   Introduction; Begin Formulating Rescarch Project Ideas Trip to Washington Elementary School

1/21   Scientific Method
          Present Tentative Research Topics in Discussion Groups

1/28   Sampling - Cricket Grooming Behavior
          Have Research Topic Approved
          Set up Appointment wi Statistician
          Turn in Preliminary Supply List to Rob

2/4   Present Project Proposal to Class & SubmiL Proposal Draft Submit Final Supply List to Rob

2/11   Turn in Final Proposal with Statistics Planned & References Cited
          BEGIN RESEARCH PROJECT

2/18   Research Project

2/25	Research Project
3/4	Research Project
3/11	Research Project
3/18	Research Project
3/25	Spring Break
4/1	Research Project; Submit Poster Abstract
4/8	COMPLETE RESEARCH PROJECT
	Turn in Approved Poster Abstract
4/15	Work on Posters
4/22	Current Literature to Apply Alcock, Ch. 15 & 16
4/29	Present Student Research Talks & Turn in Papers

POINTS DISTRIBUTION (400 Points)

Scientific Method	10
Sampling Exercise	25
Semester Project	
Oral Proposal	40
Written Proposal	50
Poster	100
Research Paper	100
Talk	75

Virginia STEP: Evidence That Service-Learning Can Enhance a College Biology Program

by Alan Raflo

When the Service-Learning Center was created at Virginia Tech (Blacksburg, Virginia) in 1995, University President Paul Torgersen described service-learning as a way for "students [to] integrate their academic efforts with practical, need-based programs that will serve the greater community." Rachel Parker-Gwin, a sociology professor at Virginia Tech, has stated that "service-learning pushes my students beyond what they know and allows them to gain knowledge outside of the classroom." And Lori Harmon, a student at Virginia Tech in 1995, said of her experience working at an elementary school: "I really feel like I'm making a difference." (All quotes are from the Virginia Tech Service-Learning Center's *Newsletter*, February 1995, pp. 3-4.)

From comments such as these, I see three conditions that a service-learning project must meet to be a valuable part of a college or university:

1. It is relevant to a curriculum or to specific courses.

2. It results in identifiable learning that would otherwise probably not occur.

3. It provides real, needed service (increasing student interest and motivation and thereby learning).

Can service-learning meet these three conditions in the context of a college or university *biology* program? This paper presents evidence that it can. The evidence comes from the Virginia STEP program.

The Virginia STEP Program, 1986-1998

Service Training for Environmental Progress (STEP) is an environmental service-learning program at Virginia Tech. It is based in the Virginia Water Resources Research Center and operates in partnership with the Virginia Tech Service-Learning Center. Through STEP, students work in communities that have perceived environmental problems and limited resources for addressing these problems. STEP service-learners seek to provide credible, neutral (nonpartisan) analyses of environmental problems and the community effects of such problems. In the process, students seek to develop their own scientific, communication, and project management skills.

Modeled after a similar program at Vanderbilt University, STEP began in 1985 (it was originally called the Virginia Student Environmental Health Project, or STEHP). Since then, STEP has coordinated 44 projects involving 63 students living and working in 35 localities. Most project sites have been in Virginia. Three projects were done at the request of a sponsoring community group.

STEP assigns students to projects based on students' skills and interests. All STEP service-learners receive ongoing training in technical procedures, laboratory support, and orientation to the community in which they will work. At the end of their project, the students write a detailed report of their research findings and present their findings to the host community or sponsoring organization.

STEP projects from 1986 to 1997 involved four areas of community concerns: drinking water supplies, groundwater quality, surface water quality, and landfills and solid waste management. The sample of titles (opposite), grouped within these four areas, shows the range of projects and geographical areas involved.

Program Management and Costs

Most STEP projects have been done as 10-week (40 hours per week) summer internships, with the students living in the community involved. Some projects have had two or three students, while others have had only one. Most STEP students have been senior undergraduates or recent postbaccalaureates, while a few have been graduate students.

In conjunction with the Virginia Tech Service-Learning Center, STEP is moving toward adding opportunities for projects that can be completed as part of a semester course. The student commitment will be approximately 10 hours per week. Starting in summer 1999, STEP expected its summer projects to be offered in conjunction with an environmental problem-solving course, held during Virginia Tech's new (in 1998) "Maymester."

For 1998-99, the estimated cost per summer student was approximately $5,000. Typically, the local sponsor provided room and board, with the program covering other costs, including a stipend or wages for the student of approximately $2,000. For a semester-based project (with the student not living in the community being served), the current estimated per-student cost is approximately $600. The current estimate for year-round administrative costs is approximately $49,000. This assumes a summer program level of six students and includes salaries for a faculty director at 5 percent full-time equivalent (FTE), a program coordinator at 50 percent FTE, a secretary at 10 percent FTE, and a full-time field coordinator. (For a detailed budget estimate, contact the author.)

For the foreseeable future, STEP plans to continue a strong focus on water quality and drinking water issues. This focus is consistent with STEP's institutional home (the Virginia Water Resources Research Center), with the

Sample of Projects Addressing Community Environmental Concerns

Drinking Water

Bald, Kevin, and Sharon Nuckols. (1990). A Drinking Water Quality and Economic Survey of Dishner's Valley and Haler's Gap, Virginia (Washington County).

Curran, Christopher. (1995). Study of the Shallow Well Conditions and Drinking Water Quality of the Water Table Aquifer in Lancaster County, Virginia.

Expose, Everett, Melissa Schuster, and Eric Snider. (1988). Lead Concentrations in the Soil and Drinking Water in the East End of Richmond, Virginia.

Groundwater

Sandberg, Scott, and Craig Smith. (1986). An Assessment of the Potential for Groundwater Contamination in the Blue Ridge Mountains of Clarke County, Virginia.

Thomas, Libby. (1988). Water Quality Evaluation in Five Areas of Dickenson County, Virginia.

Surface Water Quality

Block, Andrew, and Paul Mariner. (1986). A Case Study of Water Quality in the Chester Area (Chesterfield County, Virginia).

Caldwell, Fontaine, and Rob Mercure. (1988). A Base Study of the Effects of Appalachian Treatment Systems and Untreated Sewage on the Elk River in Sutton, West Virginia.

Sigler, James. (1991). Nonpoint Source Pollution: An Analysis of the Chestnut Creek Watershed (Carroll and Grayson Counties, and the City of Galax, Virginia).

Worley, Bethany, and Cheryl Cobb. (1989). Developing a Monitoring Network on the Rappahannock River (Fauquier, King George, and Stafford Counties, and the City of Fredericksburg, Virginia).

Landfills and Solid Waste Management

Bell, Clifton, and Jacqueline Horsey. (1988). A Study of Four West Virginia Landfills and a Proposed Landfill and Their Effects on Nearby Wells

Humphreys, Elizabeth, and George Shaler. (1986). An Assessment of Solid Waste Management in King and Queen County (Virginia).

Slifer, Dennis. (1986). Rockbridge County (Virginia) Waste Disposal Sites and Their Potential for Water Contamination.

current emphasis in Virginia on a number of water-related issues (such as the impacts of nonpoint source pollution on the Chesapeake Bay), and with requests received from communities.

How Virginia STEP Meets the Three Conditions

Relevance to a Biology Program

A service-learning project should be "relevant" to a biology program if it involves the use of scientific skills or the analysis of scientific issues that reinforces material covered by one or more courses in the program. The biology program at Virginia Tech — a well-established and well-respected state university — provides a reasonable test case. The table *opposite* identifies six undergraduate or graduate courses in the Virginia Tech program to which one or more STEP projects between 1986 and 1997 would be relevant. (These projects were *not* actually done as part of the courses listed; these examples are intended to show their potential for relevance.) While not all past STEP projects would fit within the context of the biology program, history shows that service-learning projects can indeed be relevant to a wide range of university biology courses.

Identifiable Learning

As noted above, Virginia STEP students are expected to complete a written final report on their project. These reports typically contain an introduction to the community and the issues at hand, the methods and results of the student's fieldwork, interpretation and discussion of the results, and suggestions for further study or follow-up. The completed reports provide evidence that, by the end of their project, most STEP students have the ability to explain the background of a community issue or need, to manage a set of research objectives addressing the issue, and to document their work in a way that is useful to the particular community being served. This does not, of course, prove the students actually learned these skills *as a result* of their project. Pre- and postproject surveys of student skills will be needed to help clarify the impact of the projects themselves on student skills. On the other hand, because most students have worked in a location new to them, the report does demonstrate that they learned and interpreted considerable information about their host community and about the particular environment in which they worked.

Evidence of student learning from the projects comes from essays by students on their personal project experiences, as well as letters students have written to the STEP staff following their project. In these records, students describe learning scientific information and skills as well as developing abilities to organize work, make decisions, communicate orally and in

Sample STEP service-learning projects relevant to courses from Virginia Tech's biology program

Course	Course Description Excerpt	Example of Relevant STEP Project
4004 Freshwater Ecology	"Interactions of physical, chemical, biological properties of fresh-water ecosystems."	A Limnological Survey of Lake Laura (1990): The student analyzed physical, chemical, and biological data from the lake and its watershed.
4154 Microbiology of Aquatic Systems	"Emphasis on ... polluted natural systems, and microbial water quality standards."	Nelson County Water Testing Program (1991): The students tested wells bacterial contamination, based on Virginia water-quality standards, and investigated sources of contamination.
4354 Aquatic Entomology	"A comprehensive course on the taxonomy and ecology of aquatic insects"	A Water Quality Survey of the North Fork of the Shenandoah River (1989): The students measured diversity of aquatic insect communities.
4675 Pathogenic Bacteriology	"Characteristics of Bacteria that cause human disease ... [and] epidemiology."	Study of the Shallow Well Conditions and Drinking Water Quality ... in Lancaster County (1995): The student investigated bacterial contamination of wells.
5044 Aquatic Ecotoxicology	"Techniques for evaluating polluted aquatic ecosystems...."	Nonpoint Source Pollution: An Analysis of the Chestnut Creek Watershed (1991): The student took water samples to be analyzed for various contaminants, and interpreted the results.
5054 Hazard Evaluation of Toxic Chemicals	"Discussion of philosophical issues in the development of standards for control of toxic chemicals in freshwater...."	Community Health and PCB Exposure in Minden, West Virginia (1989): The chemicals in freshwater..." students surveyed soil near a stream for PCBs and conducted a health survey for possible effects of long-term PCB exposure.

Note: All projects listed were done over approximately 10 weeks in summer.

writing, and work with people different from themselves. The following quotations from student documents describe their accomplishments in learning science-related information or skills, and in developing an understanding of the social aspects of science-related issues.

I have been exposed to the entire realm of environmental legislation and regulation covering [land, air, and water]. . . . I [now] know the most commonly used technologies to dispose of, and prevent migration of, waste. Further, I know what types of elements are likely to migrate under varying conditions. I have learned what effects different concentrations of certain elements can have on human health. . . . I [now] know what types of instruments are used for chemical analyses [and] . . . the general range of operating costs for the test.

The educational aspects of the internship only began with learning about the specific environmental problem facing the communities I worked in. It was very enlightening to see how politics, community organization, environmental law, and scientific knowledge relate in the scenario of solving environmental problems.

Topics ranging from community politics to environmental law to scientific analysis of water were studied, giving me an incredible breadth of exposure to the environmental field. . . .

This internship taught me a lot about the environment and policy concerning the environment that cannot be learned in a classroom. Hands-on experience in the field and in the laboratory helped me better understand how the environment works and is threatened. Working with [the community group and the community] taught me a great deal about environmental policy and the problems communities face from those policies. . . .

While these comments do not prove that science-related service-learning projects will invariably result in significant scientific learning, they do show that projects can result in learning that is relevant to a science program and that students identify as relevant to themselves.

Provision of Needed Service

All past STEP projects have been done at the request of one or more groups of citizens living or working in the community of interest. Requesting groups have included nonprofit organizations, local and regional governments, and ad hoc groups of concerned citizens. Consequently, the service requested was clearly needed, or at least perceived to be needed, by at least some segment of the local community. In addition, many groups that needed a project done lacked sufficient financial resources so that a low-cost program such as STEP was particularly beneficial.

What evidence indicates that the STEP projects have actually delivered the needed services? The primary source of such evidence is the students' final project reports, along with accompanying background material in the project files, such as newspaper articles, information provided by the requesting groups, and data records. These records, as summarized by past STEP directors in annual reports to STEP's advisory council, indicate two things: (1) that students typically established reasonable objectives consistent with the community need (as expressed in the requesting letters or news articles); and (2) that students generally met the stated objectives.

Other evidence that STEP students have provided needed service has come from comments by community group members, usually in letters to the STEP staff. The following is a sample of those comments.

> The study . . . has afforded the Richmond East End community the opportunity to address concerns that have plagued the community for a long time. . . . [We] thank you . . . for the study and for the human development of our community because of the results.

> The project . . . had a major impact in increasing local community awareness of what a valuable resource the North Fork of the Shenandoah River is. . . . Your professional report will give our organization a sorely needed benchmark of scientific data necessary for future scientific studies and monitoring of the River. . . .

> The study . . . was valuable for several reasons. First, Nelson County can now point to evidence that water quality problems can be associated with some of their allowable land uses as well as non–land use variables (such as well type). Additionally, baseline information for future environmental surveys has been established. Finally, the very act of providing well-thought-out data for the county's policy document will demonstrate the value of data for future county needs.

> In dollars and cents where they can be measured, the value of his internship was about $10,000. But there is no way to put a price tag on the future of children we will be able to save from lead poisoning and E. coli bacteria in their wells. Nor can we put a price on the knowledge we now have for our work with shallow wells. The families that now know that their wells are safe from a kerosene spill would like me to extend their thanks.

This sample should not be taken to suggest that all STEP projects were completely successful and generated similar comments. However, it does provide evidence that many STEP students and projects met science-related needs perceived as very real by the requesting community group.

Weighing the Evidence

I have presented this information about STEP as evidence that service-learning has the potential to enhance the education of students in a college or university biology program. That potential rests on a service-learning project's meeting three conditions: relevance to the institution's biology program; identifiable student learning as a result of the project; and real, needed service provided by the project. The history of the STEP program shows that service-learning projects can meet those three conditions.

Perhaps a final caution is in order. Despite service-learning's potential, it will not necessarily fit into every college or university biology program. To a large extent, the fit depends on whether faculty and students have the capacity and interest to respond to the particular needs of the citizens served by the institution. But a reasonable judgment is that there is no fundamental — that is, discipline-specific — reason why biology and service-learning cannot be partners.

Service-Learning in Biology: Providing a College Experience for High School Students

by Scott S. Kinnes

After several years of refining the concept described below, the Biology Community Outreach Program at Azusa Pacific University has developed into an effective way to incorporate service-learning into the second semester of the two-semester first-year sequence for biology majors. The following elements make the program successful:

1. selection of topics applicable to material covered in the course

2. use of paying, private community groups, such as home schoolers, to financially support the program

3. outreach to public community groups, such as high schools and middle schools

4. use of service-learning interns to supervise the entire project

5. well-established procedures, deadlines, and forms to guide the college students preparing the labs

6. coordination with the university's admissions office to provide underrepresented high school students with further exposure to university life through a campus tour and lunch in the cafeteria.

While this type of program may not be applicable to a larger institution where class size is in the hundreds, it certainly works well with classes of fewer than 50. It could also be one of several options offered to students in a larger biology class.

Background

Azusa Pacific University is a comprehensive university located 25 miles northeast of Los Angeles. It currently has approximately 2,500 undergraduate and 2,500 graduate students enrolled in one college and five schools. While service-learning is a relatively new interest, the university has a long-standing tradition of reaching out to the community, a tradition rooted in its identity as an interdenominational Christian university. Students are required to complete 120 hours of "ministry credits" for graduation, and a variety of opportunities exist to allow students to fulfill this requirement. Occasionally, these opportunities are tied to a course-related experience.

The Department of Biology and Chemistry has participated in this type of experience since the mid 1980s, when it sponsored a regional science fair and created a series of lab demonstrations for presentation at local public schools. Students assisted in both these efforts.

The department's longest-running program is a medical missions program, Team Luke, that has conducted clinics in Mexico for the past 11 years. Run by pre-med and nursing majors, this trip gives participants valuable hands-on medical experience while providing urgent medical care for local populations. However, up until two years ago when a medical missions class was formed for students participating in Team Luke, none of these service efforts was directly related to classwork, and therefore the learning potential of the efforts was not developed.

Home Schooling Connection

In 1994 an effort was made to incorporate community service into classes to enhance student learning in a unique way. A number of factors helped make this type of service-learning possible. One is the rich tradition and expectation of community service that exist on campus. Another is small class size, which requires only a few associations with community groups in order to provide opportunities for all participating students. Finally, due to the large number of professors who home school their children, our ties with that community group have been very strong.

In fact, this last factor was the initial motivation for beginning the Biology Community Outreach Program in 1994. My wife and I have elected to home school our own two children, and we are members of a local independent study program that includes approximately 150 K-8 students. In this group, parents with specialized backgrounds frequently conduct classes in their areas of expertise, charging participants for attending the classes. It was therefore logical for me to offer a science program to this group.

The advantages of working with a home school group, now present in virtually all communities, are numerous. Home school parents are highly motivated to participate in projects such as my science program because science is the most difficult area for them to teach. Furthermore, these parents tend to be very involved with their children, and the latter are well disciplined and very easy to work with. This is an important consideration wherever lab equipment, reagents, etc., are being used. Also, home school students are available at virtually any time that space is available at the university. However, perhaps the most important factor has been that this group is perfectly willing, and accustomed, to pay for the privilege of attending such classes. These fees have provided such a substantial income to support the project that we were eventually able to host public high school groups on a 2:1 ratio with home school groups.

Initial Efforts

The initial experiment in inviting an off-campus group to attend lab classes at our facilities occurred in spring 1994. Details were first worked out with our university attorneys to ensure that liabilities and responsibilities would be properly handled. As a result, liability release and emergency care forms were created. After arranging for a suitable time, lab space, and a student assistant, we placed an ad for the program in the newsletter of one of the area's larger community home school groups. Within days of its appearance, all spaces were full and a waiting list was started. I myself taught this first program over the course of a semester, meeting every other week — an Introduction to Biology lab for fourth and fifth graders. The student assistant chosen to help had indicated an interest in eventually teaching science at the elementary level. She was paid from the $5.00 per session each child was charged, and this fee also covered the cost of the limited supplies used.

With the success of this first experience and my own growing familiarity with such work, I applied for an in-house grant under a Council of Independent Colleges award Azusa Pacific had received to fund service-learning projects. The grant provided funds to allow me to develop service-learning components for my 300-level Ecology and 100-level General Biology II courses and to hire several service-learning interns to assist me. Both opportunities proved essential to the success of the program. My ability to spend time during the summer of 1994 in thinking through how the new service-learning components would fit into the courses, how students would be graded, what topics would be covered, and how both service and learning components would be structured was critically important. Having time to prepare also gave me an opportunity to find a local high school teacher who would be willing and able to participate in the program. Of equal importance, service-learning interns freed me from having to assist each course participant in creating a two-hour lab program and from having to be present at each lab presentation in order to grade student presentations. The interns also provided back-up and assistance to the student presenter during lab sessions.

As a trial run, students in Ecology held seven classes, every two weeks, for a group of fourth- and fifth-grade home schoolers during the fall of 1994. The topics revolved around environmental science. Each Ecology student was required to meet with me to rough out how the topic would be handled. Labs were to contain some lecture but be mostly hands-on activities incorporating computers, laser disks, a variety of typical lab materials, and, where appropriate, field trips. Students then met with the service-learning interns, who assisted them in developing a curriculum, finding material, and organizing the lab. A grading sheet was eventually developed to ensure consistency and to show students how they would be graded. While we learned much regarding the in's and out's of such a program, even our initial results were encouraging. The home school students enjoyed the experience, and their parents were very pleased with an opportunity for extracurricular science experiences. The college students, while initially dismayed at the prospect of having to prepare and present a two-hour lab to real students, were generally enthusiastic and said they learned a lot about the topic they covered and about what was required to teach such a lab. The interns also gained valuable experience relative to their careers in teaching.

With this experience behind us, we felt ready to tackle a larger group and to reach out to our real target audience, the public schools. Efforts were made to find a district, principal, and teacher willing to participate in the program. This took considerable effort; although many teachers were interested in bringing their class to campus, some did not want to come more than once, some could not get permission to do so from their principal or district, and still others could not afford the transportation. Fortunately, Azusa has a good working relationship with Azusa Unified School District, and details were eventually worked out allowing a group of 15 high school students to participate in seven labs during the spring 1995 semester.

In light of our initial experience, the service-learning interns and I developed more stringent requirements regarding a number of items. Forms were created and deadlines set for student lab instructors to notify us of the material and supplies they would need for their labs far enough in advance to ensure that missing items could be ordered on time. Detailed outlines of exactly what the college students were going to do were required between the time they met with me and the interns, and when their labs were held, thus allowing interns to suggest alternatives whenever necessary. And finally, penalties were incorporated for failing to follow established procedures.

With these improvements in place, a more ambitious program was created whereby a group of high school and a group of home school students attended on alternating weeks. The focus of this series of labs was human biology, which dealt primarily with the material the college students had had in the first part of General Biology during the previous semester. At the conclusion of the series, the high school students were treated to lunch at the university cafeteria and a university T-shirt. The admissions office provided a campus tour.

Program Expansion

The success of this semester led to our writing a grant proposal under the California Campus Compact's Science, Engineering, Architecture, Mathematics, and Computer Science (SEAMS) program. While the sum applied for was modest (approximately $3,500), it provided for the expansion of the program in two areas. During the summer of 1995, I spent time working with one of our physics professors to incorporate a service-learning component into his 200-level Fundamentals of Physics course. Work was also done to retool the General Biology II service-learning component to allow participation by an Advanced Placement high school group. Finally, a new curriculum was developed to provide a kingdom survey over the course of the semester. The grant monies covered stipends for the two professors, several service-learning interns' salaries, transportation for the high school students, and a portion of the supplies required. The latter was also met through the fee charged the home school group.

The physics component, conducted during the fall of 1995, was not considered a success by the participating professor. In hindsight, we realized we had allowed insufficient time to establish a working relationship with the schools willing to come to campus. As a result, we ended up working with several high school classes at their home sites. Under these circumstances, the service-learning interns hired to assist were unable to provide as much support as was necessary. Hence, the professor had to do even more work and attend each session to grade the college students. Much of the difficulty encountered here was due to the professor's inexperience in dealing with this type of project — specifically, in not allowing adequate time prior to the start of the semester to prepare for the program.

However, the biology component of the spring 1996 program was a great success. It reached a wider audience and ran more smoothly than ever before. Service-learning interns, university students, and high school students all enjoyed the program and felt they had benefited from it, with students devoting approximately 10 hours of work to their presentations. The high school teachers were particularly pleased with the program, as they were able to provide their students with lab experiences the students would otherwise never have had while simultaneously introducing them, perhaps for the first time, to the idea of attending college. The Advanced Placement class benefited, since the regular curriculum did not allow time for coverage of the kingdoms, an important part of such a class. Both high school groups enjoyed the campus tour and lunch at the cafeteria.

Project Evaluation

As required by the granting agency, an outside evaluator, the university's Office of Service-Learning, and I conducted surveys. They assessed the impact the program had on participating students' perceptions of service-learning and on what they and the high school students had learned in preparing and taking the labs. In order to compare similar classes, we also surveyed a general studies biology course for nonmajors not involved in this project.

Surveys used to evaluate the impact of the *service* component on the university students demonstrated that Azusa students have a rich tradition, frequently dating back to junior high and high school, of service to others. Of the 27 students in the class not participating in the project, 96 percent had provided service to others in a volunteer capacity prior to college. Seventy-five percent of the 20 students involved in the project had also had previous service experience. Involvement in civic, school, or church service projects was thus the rule rather than the exception. Hence, for this group of students, participating in a service-learning project did not greatly impact their opinion of or interest in serving others. However, survey results did indicate that participating in the project clearly helped the students appreciate how their chosen discipline could empower them to serve others in new ways. The project enabled many of them to begin to see that their science major could and would allow them to provide other services to their community and developed in them an awareness that this should be a part of their career. Indeed, 90 percent agreed that they would do so. The overall results of the survey are shown *opposite*.

My own "survey" to assess the impact of the *learning* component on the university students was a simple one. As part of the course's final exam, students were required to answer an essay question on the kingdom that each had given his or her presentation on. In the past, such a question was also asked, frequently allowing the student the choice of several possible kingdoms to discuss; the answers were frequently woefully inadequate. However, without knowing ahead of time that this type of question would be asked, students this time wrote very lengthy, detailed answers on their kingdom, demonstrating greater knowledge about the topic than I had ever seen before. Assessing the impact on the high school students' knowledge, however, proved more difficult to do. For one high school, a posttest covering the basics of each kingdom was written and given to the 19 students who had participated in the project and a group of 18 students who had not. Comparison of the grades showed that students who had participated in the course averaged 5 percent better on the test. Discussions with the teacher showed that problems had occurred due to the timing of the tests, the number of students able to take the test, and the fact that the group had actually changed participants during the semester. The high school that sent the Advanced Placement class was unable to participate in the comparison test.

Latest Effort

During the spring 1997 semester, the General Biology II class once again included a service-learning component. Since the grant monies had been

Percentage of students "strongly agreeing" or "agreeing."

Statement	SL Class	Non-SL Class
I think service-learning is a good way to increase my learning in the course.	94	92
I think service-learning activities provide real service to others.	76	75
My knowledge of opportunities to serve increased as a result of this course.	60	84
Overall, I feel that the service-learning project was a valuable experience.	77	91
I believe it is important for me to be involved in service to others.	95	93
Being a student at APU has increased my ability to serve others.	95	89
Being a student at APU has increased my desire to serve others.	85	85
I believe my major will increase my ability to serve others.	90	89
Being a student at APU has shown me how my major can be used to serve.	95	84

spent, less financial support was available, and accommodating the two high school teachers who wished to participate again meant creating two home school groups to help support this involvement. However, due to the quality of the university students enrolled in the class, the quality of the lab presentations varied considerably, and complaints from the high school teachers followed. When several of the university students had to withdraw from the class, presentations had to be rearranged, and several university students repeated their presentations for the high school groups otherwise not covered.

Conclusions

After three years of conducting this program, I believe it has consistently demonstrated its value to both the participating university and the high school students. While the surveys taken did not yield data strongly attesting to the effectiveness of the learning that took place, anecdotal evidence exists to support the belief that the university students certainly did increase their knowledge of the subjects they taught. Similarly, the high school students, who would never have had an opportunity to study these subjects, clearly gained knowledge they would not otherwise have had.

In other words, the intangible results that are almost impossible to adequately measure appear to be substantial. Conversations with the university students before and after their experience have consistently demonstrated increased confidence and skill in doing oral presentations and demonstrations. The students have exhibited an increased appreciation for the time and effort required for making such presentations and have affirmed a desire to go into teaching or to seek alternative careers. Conversations with the high school students and their teachers and/or parents have conveyed an increased awareness of and appreciation for biology and, more important, a new or renewed interest in the high school students' attending college.

The project therefore continues to represent a worthwhile and important program for our department. Efforts are currently under way to incorporate it as a regular component of the first-year biology experience and also to improve its effectiveness for all involved. (A copy of the course description follows.) Strict adherence to the principles stated in the opening section of this chapter will, I believe, allow this to occur.

AZUSA PACIFIC UNIVERSITY
DEPARTMENT OF BIOLOGY
SPRING 1999

APU MISSION STATEMENT: Azusa Pacific University exists as an evangelical, Christian community of discipleship and scholarship to advance the work of God in the world through liberal arts and professional programs of higher education that encourage students to develop a Christian perspective on truth.

DEPARTMENT MISSION STATEMENT: The Department of Biology and Chemistry exists to serve God through the integration of a Christian perspective into the disciplines of biology and chemistry and the preparation of Christian men and women to assume leadership roles in these sciences.

BIOL-112   General Biology II

INSTRUCTOR INFO: Dr. Scott S. Kinnes
Office: W-08
Ext.:   3362.
E-Mail: skinnes @ al2u.edu
Website: www.apu.edu/-skinnes
Real office hours: Tues. 10:30 am to 11:30 am
                    Thurs. 1:00 pm to 2:00 pm. (Other office hours by appointments)
Virtual office hours: TBA

COURSE CONTENT:
A continuation of General Biology 1. Topics covered include evolution, ecology, plant biology and a survey of the five kingdoms of life. *Prerequisite:* C or better in BIOL 111

COURSE OBJECTIVE:
To prepare the major for upper level biology courses, the GRE and the MCAT by creating a firm foundation in biology and to begin training students in basic scientific methodologies and skills.

REQUIRED READING:
Text: Biology, McFadden and Keeton,1995.-.W.W. Norton
Lab Manual: Biology Laboratory Manual, S. Mader, 1996. Wm. C. Brown
Supplemental: Biology Through the Eyes of Faith, R. Wright, 1989 Harper and Row
               A Short Guide to Writing About Biology, Pechenik, 1997
               A Life Science Lexicon, W. N. Marchurk, 1992

COURSE REQUIREMENTS:

1. Graded Material

A. Tests	4 Lecture Tests	36%
	1 Final Exam	15%
	3 Lab Practicals	24%

Each lecture test and lab practical will cover only the new material since the last test. The final exam will be comprehensive. However, essay questions on lecture tests may require, include or be based upon past knowledge.

B. Service Learning Project   10%
C. Vocabulary Quizzes   5%
D. Lab Project   10%

2. Non-Graded Material
   A. Conferences

   (1) All students must meet with the professor for a general conference sometime before February 26,1999. Failure to do so will lower the course grade five points.

   (2) Any student receiving a grade below 70% on any test must meet with the professor within two weeks of that test. Students will be expected to bring their test with them. Failure to do so will lower the course grade five points.

   B. Lunch
   All students will be expected to attend at least one of the 'to be arranged' lunches with the professor. Failure to do so will lower the course grade five points.

3. Minimum Grade Expectation

   A. No student will receive a "C" or better course grade without achieving at least a 70% average on the four lecture tests, one final exam and the three lab practicals. Vocabulary quizzes and projects cannot increase an "exam" average of less than 70%.

   B. Any student receiving a "D" or "F" will not be allowed to move on to the next level of courses in the biology sequence without further basic science preparation.

4. Other Requirements -- see individual attached sheets for details.

5. All Grading -- the grading scale is as follows:

A	=	100 - 92		C	=	77.9 - 72
A−	=	91.9 - 90		C−	=	71.9 - 70
B+	=	89.9 - 88		D+	=	69.9 - 68
B	=	87.9 - 82		D	=	67.9 - 62
B−	=	81.9 - 80		D−	=	61.9 - 60
C+	=	79.9 - 78		F	=	59.9 - 0

COURSE PHILOSOPHY

This course is designed to teach you several things. In no particular order they are: biology, how to survive life after APU, and how to integrate your Christian faith with virtually everything you do. Granted, that may seem like a big statement, so let me explain what I mean.

GENERAL BIOLOGY:
Hopefully, since this is a course entitled "General Biology II," you will learn something about that subject through taking this course! This will be done through the lectures, the labs, the quizzes and exams and the project. This aspect of the course is to be a two-way street and will require work on your part that goes beyond the tests and papers. You will be expected to read the material prior to lecture or lab and to review those sections which you still do not understand after class. I stand ready, willing and able to help you through any difficulties that you may encounter but only after you have at least made an effort to understand it on your own.

LIFE AFTER APU:
More importantly, perhaps, this course, like college in general, is designed to teach you how to survive after college. This includes life in graduate school, whatever job you may get and life in general.

1. Tests:
In lecture most tests will be 40-60% "scantron" -type questions. However, tests will usually include essay-type questions in which the questions will require you to put down in correct form a paragraph that will demonstrate your knowledge of the subject under discussion. If you omit important information, do not put the answer down in an essay format or just regurgitate everything on the subject without applying it to the question, or you will lose points. Often, however, the questions will be short answers (usually lists of some type, often with short elaborations), diagrams of something we have discussed or a vocabulary question with a list of important words for which you must furnish a short sentence-type answer that completely defines the words as we discussed them.

2. Attendance:
The first three lecture absences will be ignored. After that, however, each absence will lower your final grade by four points so that an extra three absences will lower your grade one full letter. In lab, you will be allowed no unexcused absences. Any unexcused absence will result in a drop of 10 points in your final lab grade. You are also responsible for attending the entire lab so do not make plans to leave early.

     The lab component is an integral portion of this science course experience and the nature general studies requirement. Therefore, any student missing two labs for unexcused reasons or a combination of three labs for any reason, excused or unexcused, will automatically receive an "F" in the course.

     It is your responsibility to explain your absences and to obtain all information presented during your absence. Excused absences include illnesses verified by a doctor's note and occasional absence due to approved extra-curricular activities. An attendance sheet will be passed around during class for you to sign your name if you are present. Anyone caught signing another person's name will receive an "F" for the course.

3. Tardies:
Three tardies will constitute an unexcused absence. If you are tardy, be sure to see me after class to be sure that you are not counted absent. Failure to do so by the end of the period will result in an unexcused absence!!

4. Make-up Exams:
Make-up exams will be given only in very special circumstances such as illness, verified by a doctor. You must contact me within a week of missing a test to explain your absence and get approval for a make-up exam. No early exams or quizzes will be allowed. All make-up tests will be given at the end of the semester on Monday, April 19. It is your responsibility to make arrangements with me to take the test on that day, at least one week in advance. If you fail to do so, you will get a zero for that grade.

5 . Late Papers, etc.:
If you fail to turn in any paper, project, etc. on time, it will still be accepted during the next seven days but your grade will be lowered ten points for each day it is late. Nothing will be accepted after a week past the due date. The material is due at the beginning of that day's lecture or lab period, depending on what it relates to.

6. Timed Tests:
All tests in this course will be timed. You will have a certain amount of time to take each test and at the end of that time all papers will be collected. It is, therefore, very important that you are not late on test days. If you have a disability of some type that prevents you from handling material at a normal rate, please see me so that special arrangements can be made.

7. Cheating:
If you are caught cheating on a test, you will receive a zero for that test. If you are caught cheating on a second test, you will receive an "F" in the course. If you are suspected of cheating, I reserve the right to have you take another test on that material. One of the most frequent types of cheating at the college level is plagiarism which will be treated as any other type of cheating. If you are in doubt as to what constitutes plagiarism, please see me before writing any papers for this class or consult your APU student handbook. All such incidences will be reported to the Dean of Students.

8 . Learning Enrichment Center:
In an effort to assist students having difficulty in classes, the University has established an excellent Learning Enrichment Center which has become a model for Southern California schools. It is available to assist you with general and specific study problems. In addition, the Media Center, located in the basement of the library, has videos, a laser disk and computer program that is useful in reviewing many aspects of this course.
     To encourage students to make use of the LEC, any student receiving a "D" or "F" on any of the first three lecture tests can raise that test grade by attending four hours of tutoring (individual or group). This four hours must occur prior to the next test. If this is done, the 'D" or "F" grade will be raised by five points or by half the difference between the two tests, whichever is higher. Only the LEC's attendance records will be accepted so be sure your presence is recorded.

9. Disability Statement:
Any student in this course who has a disability that might prevent him or her from fully demonstrating his or her abilities should meet with an advisor in the LEC as soon as possible to initiate disability verification and discuss accommodations that may be necessary to ensure your full participation in the successful completion of course requirements.

SERVICE LEARNING PROJECT

PURPOSE:
To give the General Biology II student an opportunity to gain in-depth knowledge of a specific area of biology while providing local K-12 students and teachers support in improving the quality of science education.

OBJECTIVE:
To create a two-hour lab experience aimed at the K-12 level that teaches some basic biological concept, to develop a "Science Career Day" for high school students or to assist in the development of a science website for K-12 teachers.

REQUIREMENTS:

1. Select a topic from the list provided based upon interest and due date. First come, first served.
2. Research that topic.
3. Develop the topic in coordination with Dr. K and the Service Learning Interns.
4. Present your project.
5. Work on your own with assistance only from Dr. K and the Service Learning Interns.

GRADING:
All material will be graded according to the timeliness and quality of work. **Failure to meet due dates will result in SL Interns doing the presentation and student receiving a "0" for grade.**

K-12 Labs will be graded primarily on the basis of attached sheet. Science Career Day will be graded primarily on organization, evaluations, etc. Website material will be graded primarily on effectiveness, use of media and completion of assigned material.

DUE DATES:

Topic Selection: January 22 (If all topics are not selected by this date, remaining ones will be assigned.)

K-12 labs or "Science Career Day":
         Meeting with Dr. K: Three weeks before presentation date.

Detailed outline and meeting with SL Interns:
         Two weeks before presentation date

Presentation: According to Topic/Group

K-12 Website:
    Meeting with Dr. K   Group meeting will be arranged week of Feb. 1
    Project completion   Depending on assignment.

Expanding the Reach of University Courses in Biology and Health to Provide Meaningful Service to Underserved Communities

by Amal Abu-Shakra and Tun Kyaw Nyein

Impact of Service-Learning on the Biological Sciences

Incorporation of service-learning components into undergraduate biology courses and related biological science disciplines has been gaining ground rapidly since it was promoted through the Corporation for National Service's (CNS's) SEAMS program. The first SEAMS report, *Science and Society: Redefining the Relationship* (Boylan and Ritter-Smith 1996) clearly displayed the interest many science professors have in bringing their scientific expertise closer to public schools, health agencies, and other community organizations.

There has been a strong belief among many that the sciences have gradually become more detached from the public. Science has become largely restricted to the laboratory. University science concentrations are perceived as "elitist" interests. However, thanks to service-learning's vision of higher education — articulated in statements such as "scholarship is not just discovery, but also integration, communication and application" (Lankford and Games 1997) — today's scientists find it easier to truly reach out to underserved communities. Scientific research is becoming more responsive to community needs, scientific research findings are being communicated more effectively to the public, and more and more scientific attention is being paid to projects seeking to bring about direct and tangible health benefits. As a result, universities have started to reexamine their science curricula in order to enhance their own responsiveness to pressing national educational needs (Boyer 1996).

The rate at which developments in service-learning are having an impact on science curricula is a function of rapid technological advances. Indeed, in this era of state-of-the-art telecommunications and advanced biomedical technologies, coupled with the public's increasing desire for long and healthy lives, service-learning has emerged as one of the best tools to break down the barriers that have long isolated biology departments and their biomedical/environmental/toxicological research laboratories from the wider community. Through service-learning, urban universities such as North Carolina Central University have started responding effectively to many of the biomedical and health-related needs of the community, participating with community agencies in the formation of sustainable partnerships and applied research (Benson and Harkavy 1997; Reardon and Shields 1997). Through the incorporation of service-learning into biology and health courses, science and health experts can help in community revitalization and the achievement of better health standards for all (Jones 1998).

Emergence of Service-Learning in Biology at NCCU

North Carolina Central University (NCCU) is not new to community service/service-learning (CS/SL). Indeed, CS/SL has occupied a central place in the NCCU tradition and mission since the university's inception in 1910 (Jones 1998). However, as in the case of other universities, until the SEAMS initiative referred to above, service-learning at NCCU was primarily associated with social science courses. Then, in 1995-96 and in 1996-97 as a participant in the Historically Black Colleges and Universities (HBCU) Network and as a leading service-learning institution, NCCU won two consecutive SEAMS grants.

The university's first SEAMS project (1995-96) resulted in the development of a biology-course-based (Biology 2700) service-learning component entitled Enhancing Community Awareness of a Serious Environmental Bacterial Disease: Legionnaires' Disease. The project was carried out using a simple comparative model in which the Durham community together with NCCU students and personnel were surveyed regarding awareness of this disease. The results were presented at a plenary session of the 1996 National Gathering in Indianapolis, Indiana, and at the 1997 HBCU Institute in Atlanta, Georgia ("Community Collaborator" 1996; "HBCU Network" 1997). They were also published in the first SEAMS report (Boylan and Ritter-Smith 1996).

The students in Biology 2700 designed and prepared an information booklet on Legionnaires' disease entitled *Legionnaires' Disease: Where Will It Strike Next?* The booklet included facts and figures about the etiology of the disease; its symptoms, treatment, and prevention; and control measures. It was distributed on campus and at various community agencies in Durham, and received much praise as an inspirational and pioneering effort to provide effective community service (Blue 1996; Bonner 1996).

For the following year, NCCU's Department of Biology joined forces with the Department of Health Education in an interdisciplinary effort. Biology 2700 was connected with a health and wellness course (CFAS 1530) in a SEAMS project entitled A Multilevel "Cascade Model" for Service-Learning Linking University Courses in Environmental Science/Health to High School Science Curricula. This model focused on the dissemination of student-gathered information on the biomedical/health effects of exposure to environmental tobacco smoke (ETS) and lead.

The Cascade Model ®

NCCU BIOLOGY 2700
(Junior/Senior Student Learners/Student Servers)
 ll   ll
 ll   ll
 ll   ll
 ll   ll
 ll   **CFAS 1530**
 ll   **HEALTH & WELLNESS**
 ll   **(Freshman Student Learners/Student Servers)**
 ll   ll   ll
 ll   ll   ll
 ll   ll   ll
 ll   ll   ll
 ll   ll   **Durham High School Science Students**
 ll   ll   **(Science Student Learners/Student Servers [1])**
 ll   ll   ll
 ll   ll   ll
 ll   ll   ll
 ll   ll   ll
COMMUNITY RECIPIENTS, e.g. MIDDLE & ELEMENTARY
SCHOOLS & DAYCARE FACILITIES [2]

---

1. High school students will be encouraged to serve the community through the programs that exist in their particular schools.

2. The community recipients who are on the receiving tier in the model do also provide a major service in return to all the students involved in the model.

The "Cascade Model": An innovative service model designed by Dr. Amal Abu-Shakra and Dr. Tun Kyaw Nyein in 1996. The model was awarded a SEAMS mini-grant in 1996-97 and was first implemented to link two courses at North Carolina Central University to Hillside High School science classes in order to study the health effects associated with lead and environmental tobacco smoke.

The Cascade Model

This model incorporated service-learning into the junior-/senior-level Biology 2700 course along with the freshman-level (CFAS 1530) health and wellness course in the Department of Health Education. The link was achieved by connecting both university courses with two science classes at Durham's Hillside High School. Effective collaboration between the university and the high school was pivotal for the success of the model. This was achieved thanks to the efforts of Kenneth Cutler, science director at Hillside.

More recently, the Cascade Model has been expanded further into the community to include elementary schools in the surrounding Durham neighborhood known as Eagle Village (Kobrin and Nadelman 1997), various community agencies in Durham, and magnet schools such as the James E. Shepard Middle School in Durham. NCCU is working with these partners to develop service-learning activities that target the schools' specialties. In taking these additional major steps toward fostering effective partnerships with its community, NCCU is also helping to secure the future of higher education's relationship with urban communities in a comprehensive and effective fashion (Benson and Harkavy 1997).

Implementation of the Cascade Model

Two graduate students were hired to assist in the implementation of service-learning in the Cascade courses. One student's primary responsibility was to assist Biology 2700 students preparing biomedical and environmental material on lead and ETS. The other student was responsible for coordinating student teaching teams.

In mounting their service-learning project, students in Biology 2700 and CFAS 1530 worked in five groups.

1. *Community outreach:* Students conducted interviews with NCCU and the Durham communities to learn about public perception of the problem. Current scientific literature and statistical studies were reviewed to help the CFAS 1530 students generate a questionnaire. The students also conducted interviews with health experts, community leaders, and concerned parents.

2. *Questionnaire:* The CFAS 1530 students used the information provided by the biology students to generate a questionnaire. All students from both courses distributed the questionnaire and analyzed responses to it. Each student collected responses from 10 people, resulting in a total of 450 completed questionnaires.

3. *Research (Internet):* Students in this group conducted a thorough search of the literature, in scientific journals and online, to obtain the most current findings on the health impact of ETS and lead poisoning. The research group

worked closely with the questionnaire and brochure groups, and was subdivided into lead and ETS working groups.

4. *Brochure:* Five students worked together to produce a sophisticated brochure entitled "Indoor Air Safety: Lead and Environmental Tobacco Smoke." The brochure included a chart based on the questionnaire, the research results, and educational illustrations. It was distributed on the NCCU campus, at the high school, and in the community, and is available to interested readers upon request.

5. *Teaching:* Students from both classes participated in teaching activities at the high school. They visited its international baccalaureate science class and an advanced environmental science class, and presented a lecture organized as follows: (1) introduction to and presentation of the questionnaire, (2) short scientific lecture, (3) "town-meeting" discussion, and (4) final thoughts and revisiting of questionnaire.

Outcomes of Service-Learning in Biology at NCCU

Impact of the SEAMS Projects

In both SEAMS projects, the students demonstrated heightened awareness of community needs. More striking, the student reflections that were collected via videotapes, audiotapes, and written responses demonstrated a major impact of their service-learning experiences in the emergence of a sense of the responsibilities that attend knowledge (Mattson and Shea 1997), and an appreciation of the need for excellence. These results corroborate Troppe's (1995) observation that connecting cognition and action has an impact on student performance and attitude.

Partnership Building Through the Cascade Model

The model has worked well at NCCU in that students have flourished within the server-learner/server-learner Cascade formula. Another important outcome has been the university's enhanced connection with the community. Since the original university–high school model can be extended to include middle and elementary schools, each additional tier allows the university-community connection to grow deeper. This was acknowledged when the Cascade Model won a National Society for Experiential Education award as an exemplary service-learning approach.

Plans for Technology-Based Instruction Using the Cascade Model

Attempts to explore the adaptability of the Cascade approach currently include projects aimed at the incorporation of information technology–based instruction in biology and health courses. Incorporation of technology will make possible instruction through distance learning, thus expanding the number of communities served.

Conclusion

Service-learning at NCCU has been valued as an effective venue for knowledge acquisition and as a vehicle of academic recruitment. Still, the journey to full academic acceptance has not been an easy one — especially for many faculty who at first approached the service-learning challenge with apprehension and doubt. These faculty were later reassured as a result of their being personally involved in peer mentoring and training opportunities available through NCCU's Faculty/Administrators Service-Learning Fellows Program (FASLFP.) This program, which originated in 1996, has made an impact on the university as a whole. With these experiences in mind, we would like to conclude by responding to a question posed by Edward Zlotkowski in "Does Service-Learning Have a Future?"(1995). On the basis of our experience, we can state that at NCCU, there is a strong belief that service-learning does indeed have a future.

Acknowledgments

The authors would like to acknowledge the leadership of Chancellor Julius Chambers in promoting service at NCCU; the guidance and advice of Dr. Beverly Washington-Jones, who has been a most powerful force behind the sustained growth of service-learning at NCCU; and the cooperation of Mr. Kenneth Cutler, whose efforts contributed greatly to the success of the application of the Cascade Model® and who is currently a partner in the NSEE project. Last but not least, the authors are indebted both to the excellent students at NCCU and Hillside High School, and are proud to be presenting this document on their behalf, and to the Campus Compact SEAMS projects referred to in this text.

References

Benson, L., and I. Harkavy. (1997). "Universities, Colleges and Their Neighboring Communities." *Universities and Community Schools* 5(1-2): 5-11.

Blue, V. (Fall 1996). "Biology Class Studies Environmental Racism." *Dimensions: The Magazine of North Carolina Central University* 1: 6.

Bonner, L. (March 8, 1996). "Community Service Is Class Project at NCCU." *The News and Observer*: 5B

Boyer, E. (Spring 1996). "The Scholarship of Engagement." *Journal of Public Service and Outreach* 1: 11-20.

Boylan, P., and K. Ritter-Smith, eds.(August 1996). *Science and Society: Redefining the Relationship.* Providence, RI: Campus Compact.

"The Community Collaborator." (June 1996). A publication of the Atlanta University Service-Learning Collaborative.

"HBCU Network Awards Four Mini-Grants to Science Faculty." (1997). *Network News Update* 1(1).

Jones, B.W. (1998). "Rediscovering Our Heritage: Community Service and the Historically Black University." In *Successful Service-Learning Programs: New Models of Excellence in Higher Education,* edited by E. Zlotkowski, pp. 109-122. Bolton, MA: Anker Publishing Company.

Kobrin, M., and R. Nadelman, eds. (August 1997). "North Carolina Central University Eagle Village Service-Learning Literacy Project." In *Service Counts: Revitalizing Literacy Efforts in American Higher Education,* p. 29. Providence, RI: Campus Compact.

Lankford, K., and R. Games. (1997). "Universities as Citizens: Boyer's Vision, Service-Learning Role." *Expanding Boundaries: Building Civic Responsibility Within Higher Education* 2: 29-36.

Mattson, K., and M. Shea. (1997). "The Selling of Service-Learning to the Modern University. How Much Will It Cost?" *Expanding Boundaries: Building Civic Responsibility Within Higher Education* 2: 12-19.

Reardon, K., and T.P. Shields. (1997). "Promoting Sustainable Community/University Partnerships Through Participatory Action Research." *NSEE Quarterly* 23(1): 1, 22-25.

Troppe, M., ed. (1995). *Connecting Cognition and Action: Evaluation of Student Performances in Service-Learning Courses.* Providence, RI: Campus Compact.

Zlotkowski, E. (1995). "Does Service-Learning Have a Future?" *Michigan Journal of Community Service Learning* 2: 123-133.

Community and Environmental Compatibility in the York River Watershed: A Project-Based Interdisciplinary Service-Learning Course

by A. Christine Brown and Samuel A. McReynolds

The southern coastal region of Maine is an area of great natural beauty and also of rapid human population growth. Many coastal towns are experiencing growth pressure and a concomitant need to plan for that growth. The town of York, Maine, is one such community. Established in 1653, York is the oldest incorporated town in the United States. Its year-round population of 10,155 grew 3.43 percent between 1990 and 1995. More important, its seasonal population now swells to more than 30,000 in the peak of the summer. In York, there are areas of historical beauty and significance as well as areas of natural ecological importance that are and will be affected by growth and development. The York River, a relatively short tidal river with its watershed entirely contained within the town of York, is a focus of concern. Historical sites along its banks are numerous, and great pressure exists for scenic and recreational development. The river is also economically and ecologically important in terms of marine and estuarine habitats. Add to these the pressures of suburban sprawl, and one can understand the great potential the situation possesses for conflict and ecological degradation.

Our interest in the York River stemmed from overlapping interests in human ecology and natural ecology, including the effects of human communities and land use practices on the natural world. The project described here is also consistent with the mission of the University of New England (UNE) — a mission that includes concern for both human and environmental health and learning through experience and service. Furthermore, the faculty in the Department of Life Sciences in the College of Arts and Sciences at UNE has had a long-standing commitment to teaching science in an interdisciplinary context (Morgan et al. 1992-93: 171). Recently, the department has extended this collaborative impulse beyond the natural sciences, and the multidimensional objectives of our study of the York River watershed have provided a rich opportunity to work with colleagues from sociology. Out of this need to examine environmental, biological, and social interactions collaboratively, we created the service-learning course Community and Environmental Compatibility: A Watershed Assessment.

(The syllabus appears at the end of this chapter.) Indeed, for many reasons, the York River watershed project has provided an ideal context in which to employ service-learning.

The watershed project has drawn on the combined resources of the students of the UNE Department of Life Sciences (DLS) and Department of Social and Behavioral Sciences (DSBS) as well as the community of York, Maine, to develop a foundation for assessing the human impact on the river and its environs. It has involved community officials, interest groups, environmentalists, professors, and students in developing and implementing an assessment of the current social, microbial, and invertebrate populations of the watershed. In this chapter we will describe:

1. the objectives of the York River Watershed Assessment
2. the structure of the course, project participants, and the activities pursued to achieve the project objectives
3. the anticipated and realized outcomes
4. the benefits of service-learning for each of the constituencies involved.

Objectives

At the outset, the project had four major objectives. Its primary objective was to involve students in gathering baseline data on the human population and the populations of other life-forms in the York River watershed. These data would provide a foundation for future planning and research directions. Our second objective was to establish a working relationship between the community and university partners in order to facilitate further investigation of watershed issues. Third, we wanted to integrate service-learning into classes across the disciplines. Our final objective was to provide UNE with mechanisms for breaking down disciplinary barriers, establishing community ties, and involving more students in service-learning and experiential education in general. One other objective that came to the fore only during the course of the project itself involved development of scientific literacy and an understanding of sociological research techniques among both sociology students and life sciences students.

Course Structure, Participants, and Activities

To accomplish our objectives, we established for spring semesters 1997 and 1998 the team-taught course entitled Community and Environmental Compatibility: A Watershed Assessment, offered as an internship for students majoring in life sciences and social and behavioral sciences. These internship students were the primary participants in the project and acted in several capacities. First, they served as liaisons between UNE and various community groups in the town of York. They also coordinated activities with students and faculty in four courses regularly offered at UNE: Community Organization, Research Methods (both in DSBS), Invertebrate Zoology, and Microbial Ecology (both in DLS). All four are upper-level courses for majors.

Nine interns participated in the program. Three were psychology and social relations majors whose only hard science exposure had been two introductory-level courses in life sciences. Six interns came from DLS major programs in marine biology, environmental studies, and environmental sciences, and had had minimal exposure to the social sciences. Their interests ranged from the hard sciences to applications of science to social policy. Six were seniors and three juniors; some had had previous experience with service-learning.

The interns presented the project and background information to the students in the conventional courses identified above. They also helped instructors train their students in the techniques required to participate in the project. The interns served as the primary agents in data gathering, fieldwork, and assessment of field information. At the end of the semester, they collated and analyzed the results, which were then presented to the classes involved as well as to the university community as a whole.

The interns' involvement with the four conventional courses facilitated several important ends. First, we were able to include more faculty in service-learning. Second, we were able to bring service-learning to more students. Including the interns, 54 undergraduates participated in the project. We believe one of the project's most important features was its inclusion of students from conventional courses. In this way many more students became aware of the activities and potential outcomes of service-learning as well as the connections between science and social policy. Furthermore, involvement of the four courses provided an avenue by which the interns, in their capacity as liaisons, could take on more peer responsibilities.

Experiential Learning Component of the Service-Learning Project

One component of the learning in the York River project was having students from different majors working together to utilize methodologies from the different academic disciplines. In this way, they were able to experience firsthand the similarities as well as the differences among methodological applications. For example, students were able to see that certain statistical and analytical procedures remained the same across disciplines.

Another important component was enhancement of the biological field experience of nonscience majors — something virtually nonexistent for years (Carter et al. 1990: 680). Given the need of many communities and municipalities to deal with environmental issues, it is vital that all citizens experience real science in the real world (Carter 1993: 140). Thus, having non–life sciences majors acquire field experience is an extremely important goal for DLS faculty. While we do have nonscience majors in the field during the lab portion of Introductory Biology, that is often the first and last opportunity for non–life sciences majors to experience any kind of hands-on work. These additional laboratory field experiences benefit such students because the students are often cut off from acquiring any additional science-related information or skills they can use in their lives or even in their further college education. The York River project, as an interdisciplinary service-learning project, has provided an opportunity for nonscience interns to get into the field (the mud, in this case) and learn how biological field data are gathered and analyzed.

Conversely, most life sciences majors do not have any opportunity to experience applications such as the process of gathering information about impacted human communities and human perspectives on the natural world. The York River project has allowed sciences majors, working with social science majors and town officials, to get considerable practice in gathering community data and analyzing it.

Data Gathering

Gathering information and reviewing published data on different aspects of both the human and natural communities of York was the initial thrust of the project. We needed to start there for several reasons. Since we lacked adequate knowledge of the history of the town, we first had to educate ourselves from a variety of published data. The availability or lack of availability of information influenced the paths we took in the rest of the project.

Data gathering proceeded along several fronts. Initial efforts were divided into two broad categories: the human community of the town and sampling of the river's natural communities. Interns from different majors participated in the data-gathering process.

Community Data: Interns first met with members of key community organizations, including the Conservation Commission, the York River Group, the York Historical Society, the York Land Trust, and the Garden Club. They also met with key individuals such as the town planner, the harbormaster, local fishermen, and small business owners. These sessions led to the development of a key informant survey that would provide data for development of a still larger, more comprehensive questionnaire. Personal interviews were conducted with 25 key individuals active in different areas. A more quantitative questionnaire was developed to gather comprehensive data from a random sample of town residents. All the interviews were completed by the interns and students from Community Organization. Analysis of the initial interviews and the development of the questionnaire were done by the interns. They were assisted in this effort by faculty and students in Research Methods. The questionnaire was administered in person, by telephone, and at the May 1997 town meeting.

Finally, the interns gathered visual data on the community, taking more than 14 hours of videotape and more than 500 still shots of points of historical, social, economic, and environmental significance. The goals here were to use this material to educate other students about specific locations and to produce a visual presentation of the key features of the town.

River Sampling: The microbial and macroinvertebrate communities were sampled from the mud substrate at three intertidal sections of the river. Samples were taken from near the mouth to near the headwaters, about seven miles upstream. The specific sites were chosen based on several criteria, one of the most important being ease of access. Another important criterion was the importance of sampling in areas where there had been expanded human use of the river for boating and swimming and use of riverfront lots for recreational, home, and dock construction. Benthic surface and infaunal communities, both microbial and invertebrate, became the focus of our sampling.

Interns enrolled in Microbial Ecology did the field sampling of mud surface microbes. These samples were then analyzed by the rest of the Microbial Ecology students during several lab periods. Initial results showed no significant differences in microbial community composition among the sites. Consequently, this aspect of the project was discontinued at the end of the spring 1997 semester.

A more extensive sampling of the river for macroinvertebrates was performed. Triplicate sediment samples were taken from each of the three sites, one to four times a month from early April through November 1997. Several interns chose to continue to work on the project through the summer and into the following fall semester. Interns from DLS led a field trip for the invertebrate zoology course on one of the sampling dates. In addition, the DLS interns trained the DSBS interns in biological field techniques.

DLS students also trained several of the DSBS students in microscope technique and in the use of dichotomous keys for identifying organisms. Samples were returned to the lab for identification and quantification of the macroinvertebrate species. Organic debris was picked out of the samples, and the invertebrates were sorted and identified to at least the genus level and in some cases the species level.

Analysis of Data

Community Data: Overall, there were three phases in the analysis of the community data. First, the students analyzed the existing primary and secondary data they encountered. An example of this work is reflected in the demographic profiles they created of the town, the county, and the state. By bringing together various sources, students were able to generate an extensive bibliography on the community, the watershed, and the river. Relevant sources included U.S. Census data, Maine state agency data, town records, interviews, and histories of the area. A review of these materials helped us to determine what directions we needed to take in further data collection and analysis. We then moved to the second phase of the analysis.

The objective of this phase was to analyze the key informant data. A student in Research Methods provided a detailed analysis of the key informant responses. A student majoring in environmental studies used a summer internship to compare the key informants with a random group of York citizens, using the same intensive two-hour interviews.

The third phase of analysis focused on the survey of 361 town residents. A medical biology major with a minor in sociology focused her spring 1998 internship on this analysis. This process involved two general steps: first, examination of frequencies and distributions of responses for the entire sample; second, testing statistical hypotheses that focused on group differences among the population. For example, responses of year-round residents and seasonal residents were compared.

In each phase of analysis, students played a key role in collecting and analyzing the data. In each phase, they made public presentations of their findings. Then written findings were circulated in the town, and local television presentations were scheduled.

River Sampling: The data from the period April to November 1997 were compiled by a life sciences intern. As future samples are gathered, this information will be added to the database. For the 1997 data set, average densities of the various invertebrate types were examined as a function of location and date. As expected, there were marked changes in the species composition of the infaunal community sampled and at the different sites. These data provide baseline information on invertebrate community composition from different portions of the river, and will be useful as the town considers development of new homes and docks for various riverfront parcels of land. The impact of development on the macroinvertebrate communities can now be monitored. The techniques and findings of the invertebrate sampling were presented on local television.

Ongoing Activities

Information provided to the town by project participants has included a summary of both data sets and a presentation to the York River Group. Since completion of the 1997 service-learning course, faculty and students have continued to work with the town on river sampling and community data gathering and analysis. It is especially important to continue the macroinvertebrate sampling over several years to monitor the impact of construction or river use changes. We are planning to expand the sampling to include a comparison of infaunal communities in close proximity to dock structures with infaunal populations in open-water benthic communities in the same portion of the river. During the spring semester of 1998, interns with the project continued to collect and analyze invertebrate samples. In addition, they continued the analysis of the community survey, and prepared a demographic profile of the town, county, and state. Two other projects included the editing of videotapes and the compilation of an annotated bibliography. Finally, as has been noted, two public forums on our findings were broadcast over public television.

Outcomes

The outcomes of the community and biological aspects of this service-learning project have been significant. We have made measurable progress in all areas identified in our objectives: data gathering, establishing a collaborative relationship between UNE and York, integrating service-learning into the regular course curriculum at UNE, and breaching disciplinary barriers between life sciences and social science departments. Indeed, we believe we accomplished not only each of our objectives but also a great deal more.

First, we directly involved more than 50 students in data gathering on both York River microbial and invertebrate populations and on the human population of the town of York. This is the largest such project ever undertaken at UNE and has led to widespread contacts in the community. Besides the students, four faculty were directly involved in the project. Thus, we believe our second goal of establishing a working relationship between the university and the community is well under way.

We accomplished our third goal of integrating service-learning into the classroom in an exciting fashion. One of the features of the project that we believe has been particularly important is the incorporation of several conventional courses into the framework of a service-learning project. Among the interns there were one or two who were also enrolled in each of the four regular courses. Individual interns worked to keep the faculty and students in those courses informed of the objectives and activities of the service-learning project and to coordinate portions of the courses with the data-gathering efforts of the overall project. For example, the two interns enrolled in Invertebrate Zoology trained their fellow students in sampling macroinvertebrates from the muddy intertidal areas and led a field trip to the river to gather samples for identification. Because the interns had already spent many hours on the river gathering samples and in the lab identifying the various invertebrate organisms in the samples, they were able to use their expertise to train their classmates. Thus, the students in Invertebrate Zoology who otherwise would not have been aware of service-learning or the issues affecting the river were shown an application for the content of their course.

We also began the process of breaking down disciplinary barriers. The results of this fourth objective can be seen in the number of students involved, the number and types of community contacts they developed, and even the coauthorship of this article.

Finally, in addition to accomplishing our stated objectives, we experienced a wide range of outcomes that had not been fully anticipated. Primary among these was the development of greater scientific literacy among social science participants and an understanding of sociological research techniques among life sciences students. As the students and faculty from DLS and DSBS began to work together, it became clear that a fair amount of cross-disciplinary training would be needed to make the project run smoothly and to keep all of the parties from UNE on the same page. The development of biological and social science literacy among the two groups involved both traditional classroom teaching and hands-on activities. Faculty from the two disciplines met and decided on a series of presentations that would address key disciplinary aspects that applied to the project. For example, the biology presentations included some basic ecology, a focus on wetlands and riverine systems, and presentations on microbial communities and invertebrates. Following 10 hours of lecture, the participants were taken on a boat trip with the York harbormaster up the river to measure river parameters and to observe the riverine features from a biological point of view.

Second, because of the broad student participation, awareness of the project spread to other students and faculty not associated with it. This awareness resulted in a greater understanding of service-learning, more conversations among faculty across disciplines, and greater understanding by the faculty of the benefits of service-learning. A third and very welcome additional outcome was a second year of funding from the Maine Campus Compact and the Corporation for National Service. Finally, the project gave us new insights into how we might use service-learning to address the needs of the Saco River where it meets the ocean near our campus.

Summary

The benefits of using service-learning in an interdisciplinary fashion involving biology and sociology are many. First, students in biology and other fields learn methodologies and generate useful results that can be applied beyond a single discipline. They get to see life applications and come to view their work as more than simply another three-hour lab.

Second, service-learning demonstrates to students that they can contribute to the community. Although they are new to the field, students often have some degree of expertise to offer. Even if their knowledge base or skills are minimal, their energy and time are beneficial to the community. In addition, as students see that their contributions are beneficial, they gain self-confidence.

Third, this process takes students from mud flats to living rooms to council rooms as the information gathered is considered in formulating policy. Such a process clearly demonstrates to students that they can influence their communities' policies. This in turn encourages them to become further involved in service to their communities.

Fourth, service-learning provides a rich basis for research and scholarship for faculty and students. Many specific student projects and presentations in a variety of venues have come out of this general effort. In addition, the baseline data provide the necessary foundation for pursuing further grant funding.

Fifth, service-learning helps faculty members develop a presence within the community. As a result, community members develop respect for the expertise of the faculty, which in turn raises the status of the university in the community's eyes.

Finally, the traditional didactic approach to teaching biology tends to convey the impression that biological science is simply a collection of facts to be memorized. The service-learning approach to training biologists allows the student to explore the world and to learn from that experience. Although this latter approach is far from new (among others, John Dewey promoted these very ideas in the late 1800s [Vandervoort 1983: 40]), service-learning at UNE has proven itself to be of continuing value and relevance.

Acknowledgments

The authors gratefully acknowledge the financial and moral support of the Maine Campus Compact and the Corporation for National Service. We also want to thank our colleagues for their participation in and support of the project. Finally, we wish to thank the citizens of the town of York for their participation and for inviting us into their community.

References

Carter, J.L. (March 1993). "A National Priority: Providing Quality Field Experiences for All Students." *The American Biology Teacher* 55(3): 140-143.

———, F. Hepper, R.H. Saigo, G. Twitty, and D. Walker. (1990). "The State of the Biology Major." *BioScience* 40(9): 678-683.

Morgan, P., J. Carter, O. Grumbling, J. Lemons, and E. Saboski. (December/January 1992-93). "A Biology Learning Community: An Integrated Approach to Introductory Biology." *Journal of College Science Teaching* 22(3): 171-177.

Vandervoort, F.S. (January 1983). "What Would John Dewey Say About Science Teaching Today?" *The American Biology Teacher* 45(1): 38-41.

Community and Environmental Compatibility
in the York River Watershed
York, Maine

Spring, 1997

A Service Learning Program

Coordinated by:

A. Christine Brown, Ph.D.
Asst. Professor, Life Sciences
E-mail:SBROWN@MAILBOX.UNE.EDU
Extension: 2462

Samuel A. McReynolds, Ph.D.
Asst. Professor, Social and Behavioral Sciences
E-mail: SMCREYNOLDS@MAILBOX.UNE.EDU
Extension: 2327

Mark Johnson, Ph. D.
Asst. Professor, Life Sciences
E-mail: MJOHNSON@MAILBOX.UNE.EDU
Extension: 2862

This course is listed as:

Sociology 300
LSC 495

Community and Environmental Compatibility
in the York River Watershed
York, Maine

Human communities and the environment are increasingly endangered in today's society. Pressures for economic growth, the world economy, and the expansion of state and national regulations have decreased local control and have heightened the strains on the environment. While this project will not change these conditions it will provide the student with an opportunity to examine the changing environmental conditions at a local level and to see how a community is trying to deal with its concerns about its environment.

This project draws on the combined resources of the students of the University of New England (UNE) Departments of Life Sciences and Social and Behavioral Sciences and the Community of York to develop the foundations for assessing the human impact on the York River Watershed in York. It will involve community officials and interest groups, environmentalists, professors, and students in developing and implementing an assessment of the current social, microbial, and invertebrate populations of the Watershed and planning for future research directions.

There are four objectives to this work. The first is to develop greater communication and interaction between the partners noted. The second is provide students with a hands on opportunity to help the community address a problem and work interdisciplinarily in formulating and addressing the problem. Third, it will integrate service learning not only across disciplines but across academic boundaries and into the regular classroom as three normally non-service learning courses will be integrated into this service-learning project. The final objective is to establish the foundation for addressing the issues of the watershed in a more indepth and ongoing manner.

There are three expected outcomes of this work. First, it will help gather and provide the community with a previously scattered or non-existent base of information on its watershed which will help stimulate discussion and future examination of the watershed by the community. Second, it will provide students with an in depth perspective in watershed management, community processes, and research formulation. Finally, it will develop the mechanisms needed for future collaboration by the project participants.

Student Participation and Evaluation

The foundation of this project is the work of the students. Students will play a critical role in determining the activities to be undertaken, the process in which issues are addressed, and doing the actual work. Accordingly, students will NOT be given a syllabus which details what they will do. The tasks to be accomplished will be established collectively as the semester develops. In undertaking this project students will be expected to perform the following tasks.

Date	Assignment	Weight
All Semester	Complete a minimum of 120 hrs.	15 points
Feb., March, April	Journal	24
Weekly	Internship Group Meetings	20
All Semester	Group Leadership	08
All Semester	Group Liaison	08
End of Semester	Project Presentation	10
05/07	Final Project or Paper	15
	TOTAL	100 points

2

Work Requirement

Each student will be required to complete a minimum of 120 work hours this semester. This an average of about eight hours a week. In some weeks the student will work more and in others less. A "work hour" is any task which needs to be completed as part of the project. These can be interviewing community members, collecting data, making phone calls, arranging for class visits, library research, reading assigned materials, and even journal writing. Hours can also be accumulated by attending class sessions that extend beyond two hours, for driving to York once a week (counted as one and a half hours), and by presenting to other interested classes. Other situations for credit for hours will be considered on a case by case basis. Fifteen points or fifteen percent of the grade is dependent on the completion of these hours. Students will be on their honor to count their hours and maintain a weekly total.

Journals

An important part of service learning is reflecting on one's activities. Journals will be kept by each of the students. These will be reviewed by one of the instructors each month for a total of three times. The content of the journal will vary from student to student and from week to week. The primary intent of a journal is to provide the students with the opportunity to reflect on what they have learned. This may include: making observations, asking questions, expressing feelings, or documenting information. The journal can also be used to record information such as interviews, data gathered in the field, or directions as to the next step to take on a project. There is not set rule for the appropriate length of a journal. If there are doubts about whether you are doing enough, give an instructor an entry or two and ask for feed back. There a total of 24 possible points, eight for each session of the journal. The points are awarded based on a reasonable attempt to reflect on one's learning.

Internship Group Meetings

Group meetings are a critical part of an internship experience. It is during these sessions that activities will be planned, work reviewed, and educational material such as a presentation or discussion of readings will take place. Each student will be expected to attend all of the weekly group meetings. At the first session we will attempt to find a time that works for all the faculty and students. We are expected to have approximately 10 sessions. Therefore, they will be worth two points each. These will be from one to two hours in length. Students may be excused for illness or work related to the internship. Students must given notification of a "miss" 48 hours in advance. These meetings will take place 5:00-7:00 PM Mondays in Decary 302.

Group Leadership

Each student will be expected to be the leader of one activity and the assistant leader of another. For example, one person will be the Data coordinator and direct all activities related to the maintenance of data, while another student will assist in this activity. In each area, the student will be the one primarily responsible for all aspects of the particular activity. Potential activities include:
- Coordination of groups
- Media director (print media, video, and photography)
- Liaison to one of three related classes: Community Organization, Microbial Ecology, Invertebrate Zoology
- Data coordinator
- Group treasurer/clerk/secretary
- Geographic Information Systems (GIS) and Maps coordinator.

3

The responsibilities will vary by activity. The intent is to provide students a clear focus for their work and to ensure that tasks related to the project are completed. Every attempt will be made to connect students with the areas of interest. There are a total of eight points for this activity. Points are awarded on a satisfactory completion of the assigned activities.

Group Liaison

Each student will be expected to be the primary liaison to one community group, agency or individual in the town of York. For example, one person will need to be responsible for coordinating communication with the Town Planning Office, the York Rivers Group, and the Conservation Commission. In each case, there will one person assigned to assist in group liaison. There are a total of eight points for this activity. Points are awarded on a satisfactory completion of the assigned activities.

Project Presentation

All students are expected to do one public presentation related to the project. This may be done individually, in small groups, or by all the interns. The presentation can be in a variety of settings. Possible fora are: undergraduate research days, presentation to a class on campus, presentation to a community group in York, or a presentation to regional undergraduate research conference. The presentations will be determined as the semester progresses. There are 10 points assigned to these presentations. These will be graded on a 10 point scale based on criteria to be discussed later in the course.

Final Project or Paper

All students are expected to do a final presentation related to the project. This may be done individually, in small groups, or by all the interns. These may take a wide range of formats. For example, it is possible to do a photo essay of a particular problem or issue. You may choose to write a section of a grant to the National Science Foundation. You may prefer to conduct a series of interviews on a topic and to transcribe these interviews into a document. The options are almost limitless. The key factor is the that the work provide you with an educational opportunity and that the results contribute in some way to the goals of the project. These are graded as a paper or project would normally be graded. There are a total of 15 points assigned to this activity.

Weekly Assignments

Because this is an experiential project that evolves as the semester progresses, it is difficult to make weekly assignments. In general, there are four phases to the project. The first will be the informational and organizational phase and will last from January 15 until March 1. The first step of this stage, will be for the various participants to get to know each other, establish lines of communication, examine the course goals and objectives, and identify the needs of the York community. For example, in this phase we will determine which students will interact with which agencies and individuals and how. The second step of this phase will include presentations by the faculty, students, and community members on key academic and informational elements of the course. For example, how do we define the research area of the watershed and why, and what are the potential human impacts on the watershed? What information has already been collected on the watershed? During this period students will make site visits to the key agency participants to see how they function and what their role in the overall project is. In addition, students will begin to collect existing field and community data.

4

The second phase will take place during the first three weeks of March and will consist of a planning phase in which the students and participants establish time frames, and objectives of the field research. These will be done in conjunction with all project participants. The task for the students will be to assimilate the information.

The third phase will go from the third week in March until the first week in May. This will consist of students gathering data directly from the watershed or the human community surrounding the watershed. These data will then be integrated with the already existing data on the watershed.

The final phase will overlap with the other phases of the project. The dissemination and assessment of information will begin as early as possible. For example, students will disseminate ideas and accomplishments through local newspapers. As the research is completed, students will participate in various undergraduate research forums at UNE, in the region, and in the community of York.

Activities in January and the First Week of February

January 20 -
First group meeting. Explain the purpose of the project and develop foundations for understanding, community, ecology, and the town of York. Reading assignments and materials will distributed at this meeting.

January 27 -
Second group meeting. Students will determine which activities they wish to coordinate and the agencies/groups that want to be a liaison to. Readings for the first week will be discussed. A presentation may be given by the town planner of York. Additional readings or tasks will be assigned.

February 3 -
Possible presentation by Heidi Kost-Gross of the Radcliffe Seminars of Radcliffe College. Ms. Kost-Gross will make a slide presentation of her groups Watershed Study of the York River. Readings for the second week will be discussed. Students will begin to develop their particular area of expertise.

5

Service-Learning in Biology:
Using the Internet and Desktop Videoconferencing

by Paul D. Austin

Typically, in the first semester of general biology lab for majors, students at Azusa Pacific University are required to work in groups on a scanning electron microscope (SEM) project. Students collect insects or dried plant specimens and then continue working together until they have a photograph of their specimen. To complete the project, groups are required to present this SEM photograph and related information on a posterboard for a grade. Students spend about 10 hours outside of lab in order to complete this project.

This assignment led to the idea for the current service-learning project. That idea was to integrate technology into the laboratory experience in place of the traditional SEM project. The service-learning project would require biology majors to present over the Internet to an Advanced Placement high school science class one of three selected laboratory investigations: (1) DNA fingerprinting, (2) bacterial transformation, or (3) cellular respiration. By utilizing available technologies, the students would encounter new mediums for learning and communication, would be exposed to the world outside the laboratory, and would be able to deliver this service in the convenience and privacy of their respective classrooms. Moreover, all the concerns related to transportation would be eliminated, since we would be providing instruction to the AP high school students over the Internet.

Participation in the service-learning project would be mandatory for the laboratory portion of the course. Students would be expected to spend about 10 hours outside of lab working on it. These 10 hours would include the time needed to create a webpage, develop a presentation, and conduct a "live" desktop videoconference.

Course Objectives

The course would have six objectives:

1. *Students will appreciate the importance of the laboratory experience.* Most students view lab as a block of time set aside once a week for an experiment. Very few students realize that laboratory investigations are designed to expose them to scientific concepts, scientific processes, critical thinking, and scientific inquiry and to serve as a reinforcement for material presented in lecture.

2. *Students will provide a community service while learning.* Instead of practicing "science" only in the laboratory, students will practice science with others outside the college community. Service-learning will provide students with this opportunity.

3. *Students will design a webpage.* Using Hypertext Markup Language (HTML), student groups will create webpages containing hyperlinks and images. Through this electronic medium, a powerful and universal form of communication is made available.

4. *Students will participate in a "live" presentation.* Most courses require some form of writing or a presentation on a topic related to the course. However, conducting a "live" presentation using a QuickCam camera adds an interactive dimension to the students' work.

5. *Students will develop cognitive thinking skills.* The service-learning project will enable students on both the college and the high school levels to engage in activities such as observation, critical thinking, collection and analysis of data, problem solving, reasoning, and the development of scientific concepts through inquiry.

6. *Students will experience intrinsic motivation.* Traditional instruction relies heavily on extrinsic motivation. This project sets the stage for intrinsic motivation by creating an opportunity for students to build relationships with one another and with those outside the college community. Incentives and rewards will now include verbal compliments, encouragement by group members, self-satisfaction, enhanced self-efficacy, and interaction with a group of high school students.

Course Process

Phase One

The college students performed experiments during lab as required. During their first lab session, they were divided into teams of three to four. Each team then chose one of the three experiments for its service-learning project. Students were to perform their selected experiment at the beginning of the semester. Then they were to present and teach that experiment to a high school science class. (See the "Group Project" handout reproduced at the end of this chapter.)

Phase Two

Teams were expected to present and teach their selected experiment four weeks after it had been performed. During these four weeks, they worked on creating a webpage using HTML and on planning their presentation. Webpages had to have the following elements: a title or banner, five hyperlinks, and three photos obtained either by using a digital camera or scanner or directly from the Internet.

Phase Three

Instead of the high school students having to travel to the college to carry out the three experiments, the use of multiple technologies enabled both the college students and the high school students to stay on their own campus. Each class was equipped with a QuickCam camera that allowed for real-time desktop videoconferencing. By means of the Internet, students at both locations were able to view images, methods, and related equipment during each videoconference session.

Phase Four

The high school students then performed the experiments they had been taught by the college students. The University provided them with the materials, equipment, and resources they needed to do so, and they were able to obtain additional information about the experiments by accessing the webpages created by the college student teams. The results of the high school students' efforts were also posted on the Internet, so they could be accessed after each videoconference session was over.

Technological Requirements

First, we had to determine the computer platform we were going to use. Fortunately, this turned out to be the same for both institutions — the Mac/OS. Next, in order to transmit video images we needed video cameras. Due to its low price (under $100) and ease of setup, we selected the QuickCam camera from the Connectix company. For our audio input, we simply used the external microphones that came with the Macintosh computers. Last, we obtained the CU-SeeMe software program, which is available for free on the Internet. This program allowed us to have video, sound, and a chat window running simultaneously. The entire CU-SeeMe program is only 600K and uses only three to five megabytes of RAM to run. (Versions of the program for the older Macintosh [68K] and the newer PowerPC [PPC] and related links are available at the following URL: <http://cu-seeme.cornell.edu>.)

Originally, we had wanted a color video transmission. However, the high school had to connect to its district server via a modem, which in turn connected to its Internet service provider via another modem. Since the necessary bandwidth was not available after being routed through two modems, we were limited to black-and-white video transmission.

In order to successfully connect the two sites over the Internet, one site had to have a "nailed-down" IP address, i.e., one that would not change. The system administrator at the University provided this address. Thus, when a college student group was ready to present its lab experiment to the high school students, the group would simply launch the CU-SeeMe program. The high school instructor would contact us by telephone to notify us that the high school students were going to connect and also launch the CU-SeeMe program. Once the high school had launched the program, then it could connect to our IP address. The result was a live, two-way audio-video conference on the computer screen. Due to the low bandwidth, the video transmission, once established, was put on pause to allow enough bandwidth for clear, clean audio transmission.

Evaluation and Outcomes

The service-learning project was worth one-fourth of the total lab assignment. Scores were based on the content of created webpages, presentations, and individual participation. Also, a survey was administered, and students were required to write a reflection paper on their experiences after the service-learning project was completed. (See "Survey" and "Reflection Paper.") Such a reflection paper is key to the whole service-learning process, since it is the vehicle that allows students time to think back on their experience and identify what they have learned.

Each student team created a webpage that contained three photos (one of results), five hyperlinks to related information, and the content of its selected laboratory investigation. After the videoconferences, these webpages were then posted on the Internet (see "mini-grant" selection at the following URL: <http://www.apu.edu/~paustin>).

Once the service-learning project and presentations were completed, the survey was administered. Its questions asked students to rate themselves on a scale of 1 to 5 as to where they were in each category before and after the service-learning project. Data from the survey (n=17) yielded the figures *opposite*. Mean scores for each category were calculated using the survey data (Figure 1). They indicate that students rated themselves higher in every category after the service-learning project compared with before the project. From these mean scores, percentage increases were calculated (Figure 2). The largest increases can be found in students' knowledge of HTML, their competence/skill in using the Internet, and their competence/skill in using the computer.

In their reflection papers, the majority of students discussed how they felt anxious and scared when the service-learning project was initially presented to them. They also admitted to being angry at having to deal with the computer and the Internet. After all, wasn't this a *science* course and not Computers 101? Students also expressed indignation about being expected

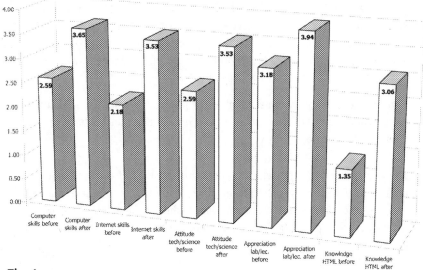

Fig. 1

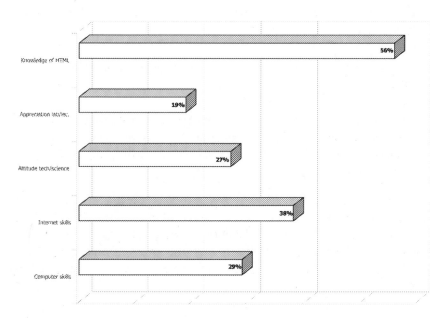

Fig. 2

to spend time on a project outside of lab!

However, contrary to these initial thoughts and feelings, most of the reflection papers demonstrated how excited the students had become about participating in the project. Teams had a real sense of pride about their webpages. Indeed, the papers even revealed an attitude of gratitude. As the students reflected back on their experience, they were clearly able to see and appreciate the tangible and intangible results of the project. What follows are selected quotations from their papers:

> Through explaining our experiment to the [high school] students, I learned more about respiration and I also learned how to work with a team of people to get the job done.

> The [videoconference] presentation was the best part of the service-learning project. It was very nice to be given the opportunity to be a leader and to teach other [high school] students about what we have learned. It was a relief to see that all of the frustration, stress, hard work, and research had paid off.

> It was awesome how we could actually see and talk to someone else through the computer.

> I learned so much and became so excited about how easy it really was to do [make a webpage] that I designed a page for my family's llama business.

> It was awesome to learn how to make a webpage and have it on the Internet for the whole world to see.

> I'm very pleased I got a chance to take part in this project, which I'm sure is unique, because it gave me a new view of science through technology. I can now research any topic that has to do with any science and get a good background on the topic.

In short, the reflection papers revealed that students were inspired to apply the skills they learned from the project not only to science but also to areas outside science. Students also indicated that they had become aware of new resources available to them through the Internet. Finally, they made clear that they had learned not only from the instructor but also from fellow classmates.

Conclusions

The service-learning project described here provided first-year science majors with an opportunity to integrate technology into their science education and to provide a service to a local high school. Through this project, students utilized multiple media for communication. These included the Internet, a digital camera, computers, and desktop videoconferencing.

Commonly, the undergraduate science experience is limited to "cookbook" laboratory investigations. Experimental outcomes are usually known prior to performing the actual experiment or can be derived from the laboratory readings. Such a cookbook approach might increase the success rate of the laboratory experience; however, it limits or eliminates the opportunity for students to truly practice science. As a result, they seem to fall short in the following areas: analyzing data, formulating hypotheses, drawing conclusions, using scientific inquiry, and developing critical-thinking skills.

Furthermore, most undergraduates function within a paradigm of compartmentalization. Educational experiences are kept separated from one another — especially in the case of lab and lecture. In other words, while enrolled in a course, students are learning topic-specific ideas, concepts, theory, and methods, yet they seem to struggle when it comes to connecting what they have learned to other areas of their education. However, through the service-learning project, students did make these connections. They collaborated with a class of high school students miles away, and suddenly science was not compartmentalized into happening only in the laboratory. Now it was also happening beyond the laboratory. Now it could exist outside the traditional paradigm — and thus the students themselves could experience a paradigm shift.

OUACHITA TECHNICAL COLLEGE

Group Project

Goals and Objectives

- to provide a service to a local school.
- to give science majors experience integrating technology with science..
- to use the internet as tool for communication.
- lab group will be responsible for a lab topic

Project

1. Create a web page with following elements:
   - use HTML template below.
   - at least 5 links to other related sites for information on topic.
   - at least 3 images obtained via digital camera.
2. Post web page on the internet (instructor will post).
3. Presentation:
   Each group will deliver a **15 minute** presentation using desktop videoconferencing. This presentation will provide remote students at another school with necessary background information about topic and explain how to set up/perform experiment.
4. Write a one page reflection paper.

HTML template for web page (blueprint)

Type this:	What the tag does:
`<HTML>`	Tells browser it's reading HTML code.
`<HEAD>`	
`<TITLE>General Lab</TITLE>`	Puts a title at the top of the menu bar.
`</HEAD>`	
`<BODY BGCOLOR="FFFFFF">`	FFFFFF codes for white background.
`<IN4G SRC="imagename.ext">`	This tag places an image on page.
`<A HREF="http://www.apu.edu">`	
`APU Home Page</A>`	This tag links page to another web site. </BODY>
`</HTML>`	Tells browser that HTML code is finished.

Evaluation

Entire project will be worth a total of 40 points:

storyboard(rough draft)	5 pts.
web page	20 pts.
presentation	10 pts.
reflection paper	5 pts.
TOTAL	40 pts.

Survey

Please circle your response to each question: 1=low   5=high

How would you rate your skill/competence using the computer BEFORE this lab?
     1   2   3   4   5

How would you rate your skill/competence using the computer AFTER this lab?
     1   2   3   4   5

How would you rate your skill/competence in using the intemet BEFORE this lab?
     1   2   3   4   5

How would you rate your skill/competence in using the intemet AFTER this lab?
     1   2   3   4   5

How would you rate your attitude toward technology and science BEFORE this lab?
     1   2   3   4   5

How would you rate your attitude toward technology and science AFTER this lab?
     1   2   3   4   5

How would you rate your appreciation of how lab relates to lecture BEFORE this lab?
     1   2   3   4   5

How would you rate your appreciation of how lab relates to lecture AFTER this lab?
     1   2   3   4   5

How would you rate your attitude toward group projects BEFORE this lab?
     1   2   3   4   5

How would you rate your attitude toward group projects AFTER this lab?
     1   2   3   4   5

What did you like the MOST/LEAST about this service-learning project?
     MOST: LEAST:

If you were going to implement a service-learning project, what would you do different?

Reflection Paper

think back on your service-learning experience 5 pts.

Discuss briefly (one page) how this **service-learning** experience relates to your science education:

- The *service* component was providing an experiment, posted web pages, and the lesson delivered using desktop videoconferencing.

- The *learning* component was the lab experiment, creation of a web page, and preparation for your group presentation.

- Reflect on you total experience ... what you thought or how you felt about this project when it was first presented to you in lab and then what you think or how you feel about this project now.

Service-Learning in the Natural Sciences:
North Seattle Community College

by Peter Lortz

At North Seattle Community College, the Service-Learning in the Natural Sciences program provides service-learning opportunities every spring quarter for students in biology and environmental science courses. The program, which began in 1995, represents a partnership between the college's students and teachers, and a range of environmental agencies in the Puget Sound region. Student service-learning experiences include environmental education at all grade levels, assistance with local park programs, trail and park maintenance, native plant plantings, invasive weed control, et al. The agencies involved include, but are not limited to, the Thornton Creek Project, the Thornton Creek Alliance, Mountains-to-Sound Greenway Trust, Adopt-A-Park, Starflower Foundation, Washington Trails Association, and Green Lake Park Alliance. Participating students have responded positively to questions regarding recognition of the worth and value in their work. In particular, they have appreciated the benefit of working with local agencies where they can see the fruits of their labor. In addition, the agencies have come to rely on these students. The North Seattle program is in large part funded by a Continuums of Service grant from the Western Region Campus Compact consortium.

History

The service-learning program at North Seattle Community College (NSCC) began as a component of a coordinated multidisciplinary studies course. The course, Seeing What's There: A Natural History of the Puget Sound, combines biology, environmental science, literature, and composition units, and is taught by three instructors: the author and Eleanor Cauldwell, both from the Science and Math Division, and Marilyn Smith, from the Humanities Division. Since the students take this course as their entire quarter course load, they tend to develop a sense of community among themselves, and the incorporation of a service-learning component seems a natural fit. The author, a biology instructor, instituted the service-learning component as a mandatory requirement in this 17-credit (one-quarter) course to provide students with an opportunity to apply the concepts and lessons learned in the classroom to the "real" work being accomplished in the Puget Sound region.

To implement the service-learning component, the instructors and an AmeriCorps member on campus formed a partnership utilizing a standard service-learning model. Contact was made with local environmental agencies, and students were matched with agencies of their own choosing. The students then worked with those agencies to fulfill the latter's missions and goals. Throughout the quarter, students were given opportunities to make connections between the classroom materials and the service-learning experience, and a dialogue was maintained among all students regarding the differing service-learning initiatives that were being undertaken.

With the early success of the service-learning component in this course, natural science instructors began looking for ways to expand the role of service-learning in the biology and environmental science courses being offered by the college. In the winter quarter of 1998, the college was awarded a grant to begin a multiyear project entitled Continuums of Service: Service-Learning in the Natural Sciences. The author was named program director. Thanks to the Western Region Campus Compact consortium located at Western Washington University, this grant has allowed expansion of the service-learning program to include up to six courses in the spring quarter of any academic year.

Program Overview

Depending on their instructor's decision, students either are required to commit a certain number of hours for a component of their grade or for extra credit, or are offered additional credits for out-of-class work (options to be discussed later). Courses utilizing service-learning include majors' and nonmajors' biology, environmental science survey courses, and Seeing What's There.

Incorporation of service-learning into a course follows a linear schedule, with the program director serving as the coordinator of all service-learning activities in the course. During the first week of the quarter, the director or course instructor introduces the students to the service-learning program. They are provided with two introductory packets. The first includes the quarter schedule and the forms necessary to complete the service-learning component; the second includes a brief description of each agency's mission and goals, the work needed from the students, and agency contact information. (Copies of some of these handouts appear at the end of this chapter.) Students also are introduced to service-learning as a mode of learning, and to the goals of the program as a whole. They are provided with a brief history of the program, and the successes of previous years. Typically this introduction generates a discussion among the students and the presenter(s) in which the value of service-learning and this program in particular can be explored.

Students are given a week to consider the agency descriptions and the work associated with each, and are then required to turn in the Service-Learning Registration Form along with the Essay Release. Both of these go to the program director, who then matches students and agencies. Up until now, all students have been matched with their agency of choice. However, this monitoring of matches also safeguards the integrity of the program, since some agencies can accommodate only a set number of students. Students are informed of their placement at the end of the second week.

Once paired with an agency, students are expected to get in touch with the listed agency contact. Most agencies offer an orientation (group or individual) that gives students an opportunity to learn more details about their work. Students then set up with their agency a time schedule that works best for both parties, and both sign the Service-Learning Agreement. This agreement acts as a contract between the student and the agency, and copies are held by both as well as by the program director.

During the remainder of the quarter, the students complete their service-learning contracts with their agencies. Thanks to a careful selection of agency partners and their compatibility with individual courses, substantive learning occurs throughout the quarter. Instructors are knowledgeable and informed about the specific projects of their students and can draw on those projects whenever appropriate. The agencies also help to educate the students about aspects of their work, and help them make links with classroom concepts. Through these ongoing links, students come to more clearly understand the relevance and importance of their work, and to appreciate what is being accomplished.

At the conclusion of the quarter and the completion of the service-learning work, students and agencies are asked to fill out evaluations of each other and the program in general. These evaluations are reviewed by the program director and used to create a yearly assessment. Students are also asked to write a one-page essay that describes the work they have accomplished, their perceptions of its value, and the connections they have made between their service-learning work and their in-class learning. In class, students are often allotted time (at their instructor's discretion) for reflection activities. These activities include sharing their experiences with their peers, and teaching to others lessons they themselves have learned through their fieldwork.

Service-Learning and Class Commitments

Instructors have several options for structuring student participation in the program. These include (1) requiring a set number of service hours to count for a component of the course grade, (2) requiring a set number of hours to count for extra credit in the course, or (3) informing the students of an out-of-class credit option.

The first two options are represented by the two syllabi ("mandatory" versus "optional") reproduced at the end of this chapter. In these cases, the instructor is directly involved in monitoring and regulating the service-learning component in his or her class. The instructor sets the time requirements for the program, and decides how service work will affect the course grade. However, the program director still remains largely responsible for coordination and troubleshooting vis-à-vis the course's service work — though in close coordination with the instructor.

The third option essentially requires the program director to assume full responsibility for the course's service-learning students. Students register for one or two independent study credits with an expectation of 12 service-learning hours per credit. Credits earned in this way are linked to the program director in his capacity as a faculty member, and are graded on a pass-fail basis.

Weighing Course Options

After two years of experimentation with the options identified above, some tentative conclusions can be suggested. The primary concern raised by students in their evaluations of the program revolves around the issue of *choice* or *control*. A great number of students who were required to complete a mandatory service-learning project (option 1) expressed displeasure with their being forced to participate. Even though many of these students recognized the value of such work, they still objected to what they saw as the extra workload outside class. (See Service-Learning Program Evaluation Results.)

Especially at a community college, instructors are faced with the reality that the majority of their students work extensive hours in jobs away from school. The fact that service-learning conflicted with or impinged upon their work schedule was a major concern of many of these students. This concern may not loom as large in settings where fewer students work full-time jobs outside class. A smaller percentage of these survey respondents noted that though they initially felt overworked, the value of the service-learning compensated for the additional work.

By contrast, students who were participating in a service-learning project through in-class extra credit (option 2) or independent study (option 3) reported a greater overall level of satisfaction with the program as a whole and their project in particular.

With regard to the program as a whole, the number of students participating would seem to have been severely affected by course options offered. In the first year of the program, two instructors required service-learning work in a total of four classes, and two instructors set up service-learning involvement as an option in a total of two classes. The total number of students in the program that year amounted to 82, contributing approximately 1,000 hours of service. In the second year, two instructors required service-learning in one coordinated studies class (Seeing What's There), and two instructors utilized the independent study option. That year the total number of students participating fell to 50 (of those, 40 were from the coordinated studies class), contributing approximately 300 hours of service. Clearly, for the program to have as great an impact as possible, a balance must be struck between maximum student participation and service output, on the one side, and minimum student displeasure with a mandatory service obligation, on the other. Perhaps as service-learning becomes the expected norm for biology and environmental science courses at North Seattle Community College, service obligations will come to be viewed by students less as an added burden.

Future

Service-learning will continue to develop as an important component of the biology and environmental science offerings at North Seattle Community College. Lessons from the 1999 spring quarter will be evaluated and changes made for the following year. The director will examine the positives and negatives of optional versus mandatory service-learning arrangements, as well as new reflection activities, and make appropriate recommendations to the college's faculty.

How to Get Started with Service Learning
Things to expect, things to be expected...

Weeks One and Two
Set it up!
- Learn about the agencies, and the opportunities
- After hearing the orientation, and reading the opportunities, select and agency that you would like to work with.
- Register for 1 or 2 BIO 299 Credits (Item # _____), and get in touch with Peter Lortz. Consider 10-12 hours of work for 1 credit, and 20-25 hours of work for 2 credits.

Peter Lortz
528-4516
plortz@seaccd.sccd.ctc.edu

- Fill out the **Service learning Registration Form** and the **Essay Release Form**, and give them to your instructor or Peter Lortz.

After you are registered and matched with an agency
- You will need to get in contact with the agency (use the contact information on the sheets provided). Be very specific when you leave a message, and don't be afraid to call twice or three times, as the agencies are very busy.
- If there is a scheduled orientation, let them know whether or not you can attend.
- If there is no pre-arranged orientation or you cannot attend a scheduled orientation, let them know that you would like to set up a meeting for your orientation. Work with them to best suit both of your needs.

Weeks Three and Four
- Hopefully, you can attend an orientation or meeting with the agency by the end of the third week
- Fill out your **Service learning Agreement** the first time you meet with your agency. This is your "contract" with them, and lets both of you know your expectations. When this form is signed, make a copy of it. Keep one for you and give one to Peter Lortz (or your instructor).
- Give your supervisor the **Student Evaluation Form** that they will be asked to fill out by the end of the quarter.

When you prepare to go to your service learning site,
- Be on time. While this is not a job, people are still counting on you to show up when you say that you will be there.
- Come prepared to work. Consider the nature of the work that you will be doing, and decide what you need to do ahead of time to prepare. Will you need to be wearing clothing appropriate for outdoor work? Gloves? Ask your supervisor these things before arriving to the site.
- Be aware of different schedules. Schools and government agencies often get holidays which private organizations and those in the business sector do not. Once you have clarified your schedule with your site supervisor, take a glance at any potential conflicts for the entire quarter, so that you can anticipate them far enough in advance.

ENJOY AND KNOW THAT YOU ARE DOING GREAT VALUABLE WORK!!!!!

Service learning

Calendar of Events
Spring Quarter 1999

April:

Week 1-2   --Handout of S/L packet to each student
                  --Presentations and orientations of S/L projects in classrooms by Pete
                  Lortz.
                  --Register for BIO 299 Credits (1 or 2) **Use item #_____
                  --Service learning Registration Forms and Essay Releases due to
                  instructors

Week 3-4   --S/L matches between student and agencies made
                  --S/L agreements due to Pete Lortz (your instructor can give it to Pete)

May:
Week 2 (3rd-7th)   --Mid-quarter check-up with students and agencies by Peter Lortz
                  (How are things going?)

June:
Weeks 1-3   --Essays (completed by students) and Student Evaluations (completed
                  by site supervisors) due to instructors/Peter Lortz.
                  --Service learning Program Evaluations (completed by students) due
                  to instructors/Peter Lortz.
                  --Out-of-class reflection activity to wrap-up and share experiences
                  with other service learning students

Peter Lortz, Instructor, North Seattle Community College, 528-4516,
plortz@seaccd.sccd.ctc.edu

Service learning Registration Form

Please return to Peter Lortz (528-4516) in the Science & Math Department
(or return to your instructor who will route it to Peter Lortz)

Name _____ Email (optional) _____

Home Phone (optional)_____ Work Phone (optional) _____

Course name and Number_____ Instructor _____

1st Choice:

Agency name:

_____

Please explain why you have chosen this agency

2nd Choice:

Agency Name:

_____

3rd Choice:

Agency Name:

_____

Please indicate the hours which you will be available to work as specifically as possible:

Service learning Essay Release

A one-page essay will be due at the end of the quarter that describes your service learning experience. Tell which site you chose and why, what you did and how you felt about it, and your overall opinion of service learning. As you are working at your site, think about what you like and don't like about the project, and what you are learning from it. This information will be useful for evaluating the program and perhaps modifying it according to your experience. Please sign below to agree to release your essay for copying and distribution for data collection purposes (optional).

I, _____, hereby agree to release my writings to Peter Lortz, Instructor, for copying and distribution as it relates to data collecting purposes.

Signature:_____ Date: _____

Thank you, and enjoy your service learning opportunity!

Service Learning Agreement

Directions for Students: Please take this form with you on your first visit to your placement site and fill it out with your site supervisor. Make 3 copies. Keep this original for yourself, and give one copy each to: your site supervisor, your instructor, and Peter Lortz in the Science and Math Dept. by the end of the second week of the quarter.

Student's Name _____ Student ID _____

Course Name & # _____ Quarter/Year _____

Service learning Agency _____

Service learning Schedule
Record your schedule in the space below. Please be specific! Indicate the days, times, and frequency with which you will volunteer.

Service learning Job Description
How will you contribute to the mission and goals of your service learning site? What are your duties and responsibilities? Be specific.

Learning Objectives
What do you hope to learn through this experience about the community and the topic of your course?

Supervision
Record the name of your direct supervisor at your service learning site. This person may differ from the person listed on the Service learning Opportunities List or the person who oriented you to your organization.

Supervisor's Name and Title _____

Acknowledgment of Risk and Consent for Treatment (for student)
Although North Seattle Community College has taken reasonable steps to refer the student to a safe service learning environment with skilled supervisors, it should be understood this activity is not without risks. In signing this service learning agreement, the student acknowledges inherent hazards and risks, including but not limited to physical injury and death, and the student assumes those beyond the control of University staff. *In case of emergency, I, the student, give my consent for emergency medical treatment and agree to pay for any charges not covered by my personal health insurance.*

I have read and agree to the agreement, acknowledgment of risk, and guidelines as outlined on the back page.

_____   _____
Student's Signature   Site Supervisor's Signature

(front)

(back)

Service learning guidelines.

1. As a service learning student, you agree to:
   a) Perform to the best of your ability and to the satisfaction of your site supervisor;
   b) Fulfill your responsibilities as outlined on the Service learning Agreement;
   c) Notify your supervisor in advance if you will be absent or late;
   d) Adhere to all the personnel rules, regulations, and other standards of the agency, including confidentiality practices;
   e) Evaluate the service learning experience at the end of the quarter.

2. As site supervisor, you agree to:
   a) Make explicit arrangements with the student with respect to expectations, schedules and responsibilities;
   b) Orient and train the student, providing him or her with a sense of the overall mission of the agency;
   c) Keep a record of the student's hours;
   d) Communicate periodically with the student about his or her performance;
   e) Evaluate the student's contribution at the end of the quarter.

3. The Service learning Program Director (or Americorps Member) at North Seattle Community College coordinates the placement of volunteers and provides administrative support as needed by the student, course instructor, and site supervisor, collaborates with the site supervisors, students, and faculty to foster innovative responses to community issues whenever possible; helps resolve any difficulties that may arise, upon request from the student, course instructor, or site supervisor, provides the instructor with the site supervisors' evaluations of student volunteers at the end of the quarter.

Program Evaluation
(to be completed by participating students)

Course Name: _____ Quarter and Year: _____

Placement Site
(Service learning Agency worked for): _____

1. Have you ever taken a service learning course before? Yes _____ No _____
2. Have you ever volunteered before? Yes _____ No _____
3. Based on this service experience, will you continue to participate in service activities in the future?
      Yes _____ No _____
4. Do you feel that service experiences can make a significant contribution to your college education?
      Yes _____ No _____

Please answer these questions according to the following scale:

1	2	3	4	5	6
strongly agree	agree	somewhat agree	somewhat disagree	disagree	strongly disagree

5. Everyone has a responsibility to contribute to the improvement of the community.
   1   2   3   4   5   6

6. The service I performed enhanced my understanding of the academic content of the class.
   1   2   3   4   5   6

7. The service I performed at my site met real community needs.
   1   2   3   4   5   6

8. This course helped me to learn more about my role in society.
   1   2   3   4   5   6

9. Structured activities in the course helped me to understand the experience I had as a volunteer.
   1   2   3   4   5   6

10. This course contributed to my ability to get involved with community organizations on my own.
   1   2   3   4   5   6

11. This course helped me to become more aware of community environmental problems.
   1   2   3   4   5   6

12. Service learning increased my awareness of specific efforts to solve community problems.
   1   2   3   4   5   6

Please use the other side of the paper to include any specific comments you may have about service learning or your placement site. Include any class activities or topics which were related to or helped you understand your service learning experience. Thank you for your input.

[Mandatory service learning component]

Biology 203 -- Principles of Biology
Spring Quarter 1998

Instructor: Pete Lortz

Office: 2421A	**Office Phone Number:** 528-4516
Office Hours: MR 10-11, TF 9-10	**Email:** plortz@seaccd.sccd.ctc.edu
Course Times: 01: TWF 8:00-10:00 05: MWR 12:00-2:00	**Classroom:** 1532

Course Homepage Address:	http://nsccbio.sccd.ctc.edu/lortz/bio203/index.html
Instructor Homepage Address:	http://nsccbio.sccd.ctc.edu/lortz/index.html

Required Texts:	Biology, 4th ed., Raven and Johnson Biology Laboratory Manual, Vodopich and Moore
Recommended Text:	Photographic Atlas for Botany, 3rd ed., Van De Graaf, Rushforth, Crawley

Course Description: This is the 3rd class in a 3 quarter series. Students are expected to have completed at least Biology 201 and Chemistry 140. We will examine 5 of the 6 kingdoms of life, and then take a detailed look at the Kingdom Plantae. With the plants, we will look at diversity as well as structures and functions. We will conclude the quarter with a brief look at the science and study of ecology.

Course Grade: Your grade will be based on:

Tests (4)	60%
Quizzes	20%
Lab Exercises and Worksheets	15%
Service learning	5%
Total	**100%**

Your grade will be based on the following NSCC scale:

4.0 - 3.5	A/A-	90-100%
3.4 - 2.9	B+ / B	80-89.9%
2.8 - 2.2	B- / C+	70-79.9%
2.1 - 1.5	C / C-	60-69.9%
1.4 - 0.9	D+ / D	50-59.9%
0.8 - 0.0	D- / E	below 50%

Test and Quiz Schedule

Date	Exam Topics (and Chapters)	Quiz Topics (and Chapters)
8:00: 4/24 12:00: 4/23	Prokaryotes, Slime Molds, Fungi (29, 30, 31, 32)	Prokaryotes, Slime Molds, Fungi (18, 20, 21)
8:00: 5/12 12:00: 5/11	Algae, Plant Diversity and Structure (31, 33, 34, 35)	Algae, Plant Diversity and Structure (19, 22-26)
8:00: 5/27 12:00: 5/28	Plant Reproduction, Growth, and Development (33, 34, 35, 36)	Plant Reproduction, Growth, and Development (22-25, 28)
8:00: 6/17 (8-10) 12:00: 6/18 (10:30-12:30)	Ecology (24-27)	Ecology (18, 28) and Project Analysis

Exams and Testing: Examinations will not be cumulative. Make up examinations are given **only** when prior arrangements have been made with the faculty instructor. Make up exams are essay exams. If prior arrangements are not made a 0% will be assigned for the missed exam. **The final exam cannot be taken after the scheduled date and time and can be taken early only with a tremendous excuse (vacation is not a tremendous excuse).**

Lab Quizzes: Laboratory quizzes will be taken at the beginning of the class period periodically throughout the quarter. Whenever possible, they will be set-up as a practical utilizing the materials from the previous lab. **Lab quizzes cannot be made up unless previous arrangements have been made.**

Laboratory Exercises and Open Lab: Lab exercises and handouts will be given out periodically throughout the quarter, and will be turned in by the assigned time. Exercises for specific laboratories will be due on the dates assigned before class gets started. No late exercises, handouts, or outlines will be accepted. There will be no make-ups for missed labs. There may be open lab times available during the quarter with tutors. I will make these times available to you during the quarter.

Service learning Project: Each student will participate in a service learning experience for 10-15 hours during the quarter. Students will select the service learning opportunity they would like to participate in from a list of choices. The various service learning opportunities and the experience as a whole will be presented to the classes during the first week of the quarter. The projects will then be accomplished during the quarter with a final paper (1 page) recapping the experience and its impact turned in at the end of the quarter. This is a way for us as **community** college members to give back to the community and learn the real world applications and impact of our in-class lessons.

Worksheets: Worksheets may be passed out periodically during the quarter, and will be worked on outside of class. Students may work in groups, but must turn in individual papers.

Lecture Content and Testable Material: I expect students to read the appropriate text and/or lab chapters **before** the corresponding lecture or laboratory. I will try to cover the majority of material presented in the texts, but time is always against me. Therefore, lecture content will most likely not cover all the material presented in the text book; however, students are responsible for material presented in both the lecture and the text books. Material not covered in the lecture, but presented in the text book **is** testable material.

Attendance: Attendance is critical for this class. Students should attend every class session. It is the student's responsibility to obtain lecture notes, handouts, or other materials in case of an absence. Rescheduling of exams or laboratory experiments should be done **prior** to the appropriate date. I will do all I can to help students who must miss class due to illness or other emergencies, but I **must know as soon as possible.** Students who stop coming to class partway through the quarter without officially dropping will be given a grade based on the work completed to that point.

Commitment: This is a course which will require a great deal of individual effort by each student. I have given you a detailed schedule of the quarter for a reason. With this schedule, you will be able to stay on top of the material, and should not be pressed for time. Attendance, attentiveness, and effort are essential for success in the class.

Teacher and Student Rights and Responsibilities are outlined in the official Student Handbook. These guidelines will be followed throughout the quarter.

Academic dishonesty will not be tolerated, and will result in a ZERO for the effected exam, quiz, or assignment. A second offense will result in a withdrawal from the class for the remainder of the quarter.

[Optional service learning component]

Biology 203.9 -- College Biology
Spring Quarter 1999

Instructor: Pete Lortz

Office: 2421A	**Office Phone Number:** 528-4516
Office Hours: 8:00-9:00 am MWTh 5:00-6:00 pm MW	**Email:** plortz@seaccd.sccd.ctc.edu
Course Times: 6:00-9:00 MW	**Classroom:** 1532

Course Homepage Address:	http://nsccbio.sccd.ctc.edu/lortz/bio203/index.html
Instructor Homepage Address:	http://nsccbio.sccd.ctc.edu/lortz/index.html

Required Texts:	Life, 5th ed., Purves, et al., Sinauer/Freeman Pub. Selected labs from Biology in the Laboratory, 3rd ed., Helms, *et al.*, Freeman Pub. Writing Papers in the Biological Sciences, 2nd ed., McMillan
Recommended Text:	A Photographic Atlas for the Botany Laboratory, 3rd ed., Van De Graaf and Crawley, Morton Publishing

Course Description: This is the 3rd course in the 3 quarter majors' biology series. We will continue to examine the concepts of biology including evolution, biological diversity (bacterial, protistan, fungal, and plant), plant structure and function, and ecology. I encourage students to participate through questions and shared experiences to enrich the class.

Course Prerequisite: Chemistry 101/Biology 201

Evaluation: Your grade will be evaluated as follows:		Your grade will be based on the following NSCC scale:		
Exams (3)	60%	4.0 - 3.5	A/A-	90-100%
Quizzes	25%	3.4 - 2.9	B+/B	80-89.9%
Formal Write-up	7.5%	2.8 - 2.2	B-/C+	70-79.9%
Labs	7.5%	2.1 - 1.5	C/C-	60-69.9%
	100%	1.4 - 0.9	D+/D	50-59.9%
		0.8-0. 0	D-/E	below 50%

Tentative Test and Quiz Schedule

	Tests	Quizzes
Date	**Topics (and Chapters)**	**Topics (and Labs)**
4/28	Prokaryotes, Slime Molds, Fungi (25, 26, 28)	Prokaryotes, Slime Molds, Fungi (22, 23)
5/28	Algae, Plants (26, 27, 31, 36)	Algae, Plants (22, 23, 24, 28)
6/16	Ecology (51-53)	Ecology (43)

Exams, Lab Quizzes, and Testing: Examinations will not be cumulative. Make up examinations are given **only** when prior arrangements have been made with the faculty instructor. <u>Make up exams are essay exams</u>. If prior arrangements are not made a 0% will be assigned for the missed exam. Three laboratory quizzes (including the lab practical) will be taken during the quarter, and when possible, will be lab practicals utilizing appropriate lab materials. There are no make-ups for missed laboratory quizzes nor the lab practical.

Laboratory Exercises and Open Lab: Lab exercises and handouts will be given out periodically throughout the quarter, and will be turned in by the assigned time. There will be no make-ups for missed labs. There may be open lab times available during the quarter with tutors. I will make these times available to you during the quarter.

Formal Lab Write-up: With one of our lab activities (C-Fern) this quarter, we will write a formal lab. This will entail a "scientific paper" style write-up with all the sections we reviewed in Biology 202. Therefore, each student will be required to submit a paper with an introduction, methods and materials, results and discussion sections. There will also be some additional small assignments involved with this formal lab write-up which will be handed out periodically throughout the quarter.

Lecture Content and Testable Material: I expect students to read the appropriate text and/or lab chapters **before** the corresponding lecture or laboratory. I will try to cover the majority of material presented in the texts, but time is always against the instructor. Therefore, lecture content will most likely not cover all the material presented in the textbook; however, students are responsible for material presented in both the lecture and the textbooks. Material not covered in the lecture, but presented in the textbook **is** testable material.

Service learning Project: Each student will be given the opportunity to participate in a service learning experience for a range of hours during the quarter. This is an optional activity with which students can receive additional quarter credits (not extra credit for this course). Students can sign up for 1-2 credits and work a proportional share of hours with one of several service learning agencies throughout the Puget Sound region. Students can select the service learning opportunity they would like to participate in from a list of choices. The various service learning opportunities and the experience as a whole will be presented to the classes during the first week of the quarter. The projects will then be completed during the quarter with a final paper (1 page) recapping the experience and its impact turned in at the end of the quarter. This is a way for us as **community** college members to give back to the community and learn the real world applications and impact of our in-class lessons.

Attendance: Students should attend every class session. It is the student's responsibility to obtain lecture notes, handouts, or other materials in case of an absence. Rescheduling of exams or laboratory experiments should be done **prior** to the appropriate date. I will do all I can to help students who must miss class due to illness or other emergencies, but **I must know as soon as possible.** A student who stops attending class without an official withdrawal will be assigned a grade based on the work completed up to that point.

Commitment: This is a course that will require a great deal of individual effort by each student. I have given you a detailed schedule of the quarter for a reason. With this schedule, you will be able to stay on top of the material, and should not be pressed for time. Attendance, attentiveness, and effort are essential for success in the class.

Teacher and Student Rights and Responsibilities are outlined in the official Student Handbook. These guidelines will be followed throughout the quarter.

Academic dishonesty will not be tolerated, and will result in a ZERO for the effected exam, quiz, or assignment. A second offense will result in a withdrawal from the class for the remainder of the quarter.

Service learning Program Evaluation Results
Spring 1998

---

1. Have you ever taken a service learning course before?
   Yes **4 (13%)**   No **31 (87%)**
2. Have you ever volunteered before?
   Yes **32 (89%)**   No **4 (11%)**
3. Based on this service experience, will you continue to participate in service activities in the future?
   Yes **34 (100%)**   No **0 (0%)**
4. Do you feel that service experiences can make a significant contribution to your college education?
   Yes **29 (85%)**   No **5 (15%)**

Please answer these questions according to the following scale:

1	2	3	4	5	6
strongly agree	agree	somewhat agree	somewhat disagree	disagree	strongly disagree

5. Everyone has a responsibility to contribute to the improvement of the community. **Mean: 1.57**
   1 (20)   2 (16)   3 (0)   4 (0)   5 (0)   6 (1)

6. The service I performed enhanced my understanding of the academic content of the class. **Mean: 2.89**
   1 (7)   2 (6)   3 (12)   4 (4)   5 (6)   6 (1)

7. The service I performed at my site met real community needs. **Mean: 2.17**
   1 (11)   2 (12)   3 (10)   4 (0)   5 (1)   6 (1)

8. This course helped me to learn more about my role in society. **Mean: 2.61**
   1 (4)   2 (14)   3 (13)   4 (3)   5 (1)   6 (1)

9. Structured activities in the course helped me to understand the experience I had as a volunteer. **Mean: 3.19**
   1 (2)   2 (9)   3 (13)   4 (6)   5 (4)   6 (2)

10. This course contributed to my ability to get involved with community organizations on my own. **Mean: 2.46**
    1 (9)   2 (14)   3 (6)   4 (6)   5 (0)   6 (2)

11. This course helped me to become more aware of community environmental problems. **Mean: 2.44**
    1 (9)   2 (13)   3 (8)   4 (3)   5 (1)   6 (2)

12. Service learning increased my awareness of specific efforts to solve community problems. **Mean: 1.97**

Service-Learning and Field Biology in Postcolonial Perspective: The Bahamas Environmental Research Center as a Case Study

by Luther Brown

The argument that field studies, and enterprises called "biological field stations" in particular, are colonial endeavors may seem anomalous in a volume dedicated to the subject of service-learning in the biological sciences. Scientists do not generally discuss such concepts, and many may feel that they are unimportant, since they lie outside the domain of scientific investigation. On the other hand, fieldwork often occurs within the context of local human populations, and frequently relies directly upon the goodwill and active involvement of local citizens.

My intention in this essay is to demonstrate that recognition of the colonial nature of fieldwork can lead to changes in the ways such work is done, and that these changes can improve the educational and research experiences of students and scientists while benefiting the communities that support fieldworkers. One of the principal types of change involves the incorporation of community service into biology classes and research expeditions.

The Colonial Nature of Fieldwork?

Colonialism is an enterprise based on the argument that one culture has the right to impose itself on others. Advocates of this philosophy may argue that their right flows from Divine Providence, that it is Manifest Destiny or a reflection of Natural Law (or even survival of the fittest), but in all cases, the colonizers act out their belief that their own culture is superior to the culture of the colonized.

Colonial imposition can manifest itself in myriad ways. Most commonly, the colonizers bring economic, legal, and social orders that benefit them at the expense of the colonized. While they may rationalize their actions by arguing that they are enlightening colonized people by their example, they are in fact demonstrating to all that the road to success in the colony is not through the traditional culture of the colonized but rather through the imposed culture of the ruler. The result of this change is the immediate and inevitable creation of a successful class of rulers — and the "Other." To the extent that colonialism is associated with ethnic and economic distinctions, the boundary between these two classes is uncrossable. Hence there is no road to success for the Other in a colonized social system.

The impact of colonialism, especially on the Other (i.e., the psyche of the colonized), is the subject of "postcolonial" narrative or interpretation. Such analyses seek to explain the consequences of the inevitable collision between colonizer and colonized. In some cases, such narratives are historical, and in others they attempt to identify effects so that those effects can be mitigated or avoided in the future.

While the consequences of colonial endeavors have been widely studied in the social sciences and humanities, they are not typical of discussions within the natural sciences. This is unfortunate, because certain scientific activities are inherently colonial. The case in point is field biology, although it is certainly not unique. Any research activity or class that is conducted in the field, particularly if presented at a "field station," may face the same issues.

Field stations are almost always located in places with abundant natural resources. Such places are typically rural, and have sparse, often scattered human populations. Such places also offer limited educational, cultural, and economic opportunities to local citizens, who have typically lived their lives near their birthplaces. These comments apply to field stations outside and within the United States and, for the biological sciences anyway, identify the reason for the field station's existence: natural habitats, meaning limited development.

Contrast the typical user of a biological field station with the typical resident of the community in which the station exists. The typical user is either well educated (faculty or researcher) or pursuing an advanced education (students). Users have succeeded in paying the costs associated with use of the facilities, and have obviously traveled to the facilities. In many cases, faculty may have traveled widely among field stations. In some cases, faculty may have obvious ties to regional, national, or international governments and agencies, and represent economic power, too. Users have their own culture of seminars, lectures, spreadsheets, and PowerPoint. They often bring expensive or advanced technologies with them, whether in the form of scuba tanks or DNA minicyclers, and these technologies may be envied or viewed with disbelief by local citizens, who cannot afford them or fail to understand their significance.

Finally, users bring new ethical values to field station communities. Animals that are known as "food" by the local community may be viewed as "endangered" by field station users who collect data from the animals for eventual analysis at their home university. Plants that are known as herbal remedies by the local community may be viewed as "pharmaceutical products" by field station users who collect the plants (and local knowledge) for possible exploitation at their home institution. And the very reason that users visit field stations is to gain knowledge by collecting information,

information that is invariably exported from the field when the users leave, leaving behind the Other.

Users of a biological field station typically do not pay much attention to the colonial aspects of the enterprise in which they are engaged. They usually visit for a short time, are intensely focused on their mission, and are typically engulfed by the academic discussions and challenges that are an inherent part of the culture itself. This inattention has consequences. At a minimum, visitors miss potentially rich cultural experiences that would be available to them if they were integrated into the community. Visitors may experience (often unknowingly) community members who view themselves as the Other, and consequently avoid offering, or possibly even obfuscate, information that would help scientific investigation. In some cases, visitors may experience open animosity toward their investigations, or even toward themselves and the field station proper, animosity that may reveal itself through theft or vandalism, or through problems with local government, law enforcement, or even the price of goods and services.

A postcolonial approach to field station activities can make such activities more productive for all involved, and in some cases avoid or at least alleviate problems that plague many facilities. Such an approach can involve service-learning in several ways. In what follows, I will describe an institution known as the Bahamas Environmental Research Center (BERC). I will explain the design of this facility as a postcolonial interpretation of the "biological field station," and explain the ways in which this design benefits students and faculty. I will end with specific examples — of biology classes that use service-learning, and nonbiology classes that incorporate both biology and service in postcolonial ways.

The Bahamas Environmental Research Center

The Bahamas Environmental Research Center is located in the settlement of Staniard Creek on Andros Island, Commonwealth of the Bahamas. Its location provides easy access to diverse habitats, including deep marine, coral reef, shallow back reef, mangrove, intertidal, and terrestrial habitats, as well as lentic and lottic freshwater sites, including very deep karst blueholes, which are vertical caves filled with water. These habitats are more or less pristine, as the human population of the island is very small, and tourism is undeveloped.

BERC was located in Staniard Creek partially because of the accessibility of biologically interesting sites, but largely because of the community itself. The adult population totals about 100. When BERC opened in 1995, the community supported a small primary school, one grocery store, and one licensed inn (with seven rooms).

BERC includes a substantial building that provides for classroom and laboratory space. It has several vehicles and boats, and standard lab and classroom facilities like those found in many North American colleges. Dormitory-style accommodations are available, and meals are arranged through BERC, giving it some of the standard attributes of a field station.

BERC is a collaboration among three parties. George Mason University (GMU) is a medium-size state university located in northern Virginia, near Washington, DC. GMU consists of several colleges and schools, many of which offer terminal degrees. The College of the Bahamas (COB) is a much smaller institution located in Nassau, the Bahamas. COB offers the bachelor's degree in several disciplines and two-year certificates in others. The citizens of Staniard Creek are the third party.

What Makes BERC Postcolonial?

Most field stations are owned either by single U.S.-based institutions or by consortiums composed of several schools. Rarely, if ever, do they include the local community as a full partner. In the case of BERC, GMU has provided management skills and start-up funding, COB has provided assistance with issues of permits, customs duty, and government paperwork, and Staniard Creek has provided the buildings that constitute BERC and the room and board support for users. This means that the physical plant that includes the classroom and lab space is provided by the community, the building itself formerly being the disused primary school. Housing is provided in the form of leased accommodations (locally owned) and rented rooms in the local inn. Dinners for users are contracted through five local providers who have modified their homes to allow groups of diners to eat in "restaurant" style. The community is thus a full member in BERC and has a vested interest in the success of BERC as an institution.

All three partners to the BERC agreement have regular input into the operation of the program. GMU and COB are primarily interested in use of the facilities by classes and, to a lesser extent, by research groups. Staniard Creek is primarily interested in regular use of the facilities (i.e., in the economic benefits) and in the services that visitors can contribute to the community. Regular community meetings held at BERC between the community and visiting classes lead to the service projects that classes incorporate. Since the three partners to BERC have noncongruent interests, projects that arise from the interaction have their own unique flavor, and rarely fit into the standard model of "service" as used at many North American schools.

There are two other parties that play important roles at BERC and influence service projects. The first is the Bahamas National Trust, a private foundation that, under act of Parliament, is also the National Park Service for the Bahamas. The Trust is currently pursuing plans to establish a new national park on Andros Island. The other stakeholder is the Ministry of Agriculture, a branch of the Bahamas government. This Ministry oversees all research conducted on land or in freshwater in the Bahamas. The Ministry works closely with the Trust when granting research permits, and is the primary repository of biological knowledge in the Bahamas. Senior members in both of these organizations provide regular advice to BERC.

How Does This Benefit Students and Researchers?

The involvement of the community, and to a lesser extent the advisory groups, manifests itself in several ways. Community members regularly stop to visit students, both within BERC and anywhere in the community. Community members regularly make suggestions about classes, and act as resource people for classes and research projects. Indeed, classes at BERC can expect local citizens to become engaged in discussions of ecological, historical, and cultural issues. The actual role that these resource people play depends on the nature of the class or project — e.g., providing advice about collection or experimental sites, providing lectures or discussions on the protection of rare species (e.g., sea turtles, orchids) or ecologically "hot" topics (e.g., cutting of mangroves, implementation of lobster/fishing seasons, sport versus traditional fishing), and the like. Government and nongovernmental organization representatives, including the Minister of Agriculture, have also stopped in at BERC while classes were in session.

In addition, dinnertime becomes an opportunity for BERC users to interact directly with community members. These simple interactions often lead to more involved discussions or projects. The upshot of this involvement is a sense that BERC users are part of the greater community, a sense that grows directly from the feeling that community members are part of BERC.

This general feeling that both the community and the academic sponsors of BERC are engaged in a common effort has indirect consequences for students as well. For example, vandalism, theft, and safety issues, all of which are fairly common concerns at most field stations, are quite carefully monitored by the citizens of Staniard Creek.

Who Uses BERC?

While BERC grew out of a 20-year history of field classes at GMU, it is now used by several colleges and universities. In 1999, it was visited by more than 300 users, about one-half of whom came through GMU or COB. During that year, BERC supported small teams of biology researchers, and classes in the disciplines of biology, geology, geography, cultural studies, art, English, and human ecology. Specific biology classes presented in 1999 included Molecular Conservation Biology, Plants and Pollinators (two times), Field Biology, Human Ecology, Islands in Biology and Culture, and Marine Biology (two times).

Where's the Service, Where's the Learning?

The services that BERC visitors render the community reflect the desires of the community and the abilities of the users rather than a preconceived notion of what service should be. Some projects are long term and involve many classes, some require group effort, and others are solitary or short-term events. All of the projects referenced below have recently involved students or researchers engaged in biological studies, and several have also involved people engaged in other classes, ranging from sculpture through cultural studies.

The Staniard Creek Library: As one of the "Family Islands" of the Bahamas, Andros lacks the infrastructure common to Nassau and Freeport. Books are relatively rare, and even the local high schools lack substantial libraries. There has never been a community library on the island, and there are no booksellers. Most children do not have books of their own, and primary schools rely largely on out-of-date or inappropriate hand-me-down texts from the British educational system. Island teachers, who often are enrolled in college-level classes on a correspondence basis, have no library resources to support their own educational goals. In 1998, a delegation of these teachers asked a group of visitors to BERC to help remedy this deficiency.

Several college-level classes have contributed to the library program in different ways. In some cases, students have collected books from faculty offices. Some students have frequented garage sales looking for reference texts and purchased them with their own funds. Many students have helped collect children's books from their own families and friends. More than 1,000 volumes have been shipped to the island, where they have been catalogued using a simple system that was developed as part of a class project. The library is housed in the local government building on shelves that were paid for by BERC. It also includes a computer workstation that was provided by BERC and installed by students.

A second computer workstation was similarly installed in the primary school for use by the teachers. Texts that are academic in nature are distributed directly to teachers who are engaged in their own studies. Appropriate high school–level texts are distributed directly to the local high school. As a side project, dozens of educational videotapes and instruction manuals have also been delivered to the local school system.

Beach Surveys: An ongoing project that is often incorporated into biology classes involves collection and categorization of flotsam and jetsam on a local beach. Classes typically record the material composing each object (e.g., what kind of plastic) and the object's original function. Many classes analyze the frequency of each material or object type, and some compare frequencies to other, similar surveys. Data are reported to the National Trust, and the minimal service provided the local community is cleaning of a local beach.

Bluehole Surveys: The blueholes on Andros are naturally occurring wells, similar to the more famous cenotes of Central America. There are approximately 200 known sites of varying depth. Deep sites penetrate through the lens of freshwater beneath the island into saltwater below. The lens of freshwater is of national importance, since it is mined for shipment to Nassau, a city that is visited by millions of tourists annually and that has insufficient water resources of its own. Development on Andros ultimately threatens this lens.

Many biology classes quantify the vertical structure of one or more blueholes during their field experience, and some focus entirely on bluehole ecology. Quantification typically involves constructing a depth profile of the physical and chemical properties of a bluehole, minimally with regard to dissolved oxygen, salinity, temperature, and common ions. Data from these classes are reported to the Ministry of Agriculture on an annual basis. Some sites are sampled quite regularly, but the diversity of sites and the remote location of many sites have to date allowed searches for "new" sites to be regular parts of classes desiring them.

Some classes have used water quality test kits to examine local drinking water sources and the government wells that ultimately supply Nassau. Results of these analyses are reported to the Ministry of Agriculture annually. Some sources have also been tested for coliform bacteria, including the water supplies of some small bonefish resorts (at the owner's request). Results of these tests are reported to the owner.

Programs, Meals, and Celebrations: The word "program" has a special meaning for the Family Islands. Programs are fundraising events at which members of the community are called upon to sing. The audience responds to the singing by tucking dollar bills under the performer's collar, and the money raised is used to support the program sponsor's good cause (usually to help an invalid member of the community). BERC has hosted many "programs," since it has a stage for performances and since it often has a large audience. Programs in Staniard Creek are important to the well-being of several people who have fallen outside the standard socialized health-care system (e.g., AIDS sufferers, who have little long-term hope within the local system).

Several biology classes have also been involved in special community meals or celebrations. A recent class found itself on the island during the American Thanksgiving celebration. It hosted the settlement children for an American/Bahamian celebration of their own, baked a dozen pumpkin pies, and was overwhelmed by the response. Classes using BERC in January always participate in the annual Conch Shell Festival. This is a half-day interaction between BERC and the community that celebrates our mutual contributions. In each of the last three years, biology students (and others) have prepared and served more than 350 pounds of barbecued chicken for the community, which has responded by bringing potluck side dishes. Several hundred people enjoy this dinner each year.

Interaction With the Public Schools: The Staniard Creek primary school serves about 40 students in grades 1 to 6. It is located next door to BERC. Many classes have participated in school activities, either as a class or through the actions of single students. For example, one class presented a day-long discussion of the coral reef, including talks about sharks and general conservation issues and activities developed by the class specifically for the primary school experience. Single students from many classes have spent a day or two working as an assistant, leading presentations on science or math, and occasionally conducting short field trips. One regularly offered botany class has become well known for simply washing the classroom windows and policing the grounds for trash.

A related form of service involves the local park, adjacent to the school. Several members of an undergraduate biology class worked together with several local citizens to build a set of swings, made out of old tires and rope and suspended from a frame made out of pine trees.

Community Art Projects: Staniard Creek takes immense pride in the community art projects that BERC has sponsored. While these projects are not directly the result of biology classes, many biologists have helped with them, and two in particular have biological aspects. One project is a large (15x20-foot) mosaic tile mural of a conch, and the other is a concrete sculpture (14-feet long) of a bonefish. Both of these animals are icons of Family Island life. The conch is commonly hunted for food, even though it is becoming rarer. The bonefish is another traditional food, now threatened by development and, perhaps surprisingly, by the elite catch-and-release sport of fly-fishing, which has pitted older and more-traditional users of the species against the younger and better-educated group of fly-fishing guides. Both projects were built by teams of U.S. students, COB students, and members of the local community. Both involved study of the species under consideration, including presentations on the biology, economics, and social significance of the animals. Subsequent classes, including a biology class, contributed further to the projects by landscaping the sculpture. This class also studied the issues surrounding the conservation and exploitation of the bonefish.

The Biology Dimension

The smorgasbord of service experiences described above includes some that are directly relevant to biology classes and others that are purely of service to the community. Learning can be involved in all of the experiences, but the type of learning that occurs is a function of the experience itself and the academic context in which it occurs.

For example, blueholes have been the focus of several biology classes. They allow integration of various aspects of biology, chemistry, and physics, and are truly a classic "ecosystem" with little material input or output. Classes that focus on blueholes must explore technical aspects of water sampling and analysis, and may also incorporate aspects of microbial ecology, plant communities, or ichthyology, depending on their focus. Such classes have no problem integrating the data collection required by the service project directly with the analysis required by the academic discussion. Extending that discussion to more general issues of water quality, threats to clean water, and problems of resource exploitation is relatively easy.

Beach litter cleanups are also easily incorporated into biology classes. They provide an excellent introduction to sampling problems, the use of transects and quadrants, and even problems of the classification or taxonomy of debris. Both the analysis of blueholes and the sampling of beach litter can be data-rich. They make excellent introductions to the use of spreadsheets and graphical analyses. They lend themselves to comparisons with other sites, or the same site at other times, and they can easily be structured to provide relatively complete pictures of local systems.

For similar reasons, at least two classes planned for summer 2000 have already scheduled time for participation in an ongoing survey of the world's coral reefs (http://www.ReefCheck.org/), something that may not benefit the local community directly but is still of service to the broader community. One of these classes is a graduate-level molecular genetics course that focuses on conservation issues, including the reef. As in the study of beach litter, survey of reef habitat raises questions of sampling, repeatability, and completeness, all of which introduce students to problems encountered by all field biologists.

Participation in the library project or attendance at a program is not so immediately relevant to most biologists, but can produce learning anyway. Almost all students using BERC maintain journals (see discussion of "learning logs" below), which are typically submitted as part of the graded requirement of their class. Some are asked to write more structured essays about their experiences. The excitement of a program, the understanding that access to information (books) can be a limiting resource for learning, or even the realization that people with AIDS in remote settlements die quickly and miserably can be quite profound, and makes an excellent theme for reflective essays. And since most faculty who offer classes through BERC support the postcolonial underpinnings of the facility, group discussions of these issues, either as part of class or during dinner, are frequent. When classes express an interest, open discussions are scheduled so that members of the community, as well as the class, can express their opinions publicly.

Some experiences may provide service, but seem superficially to lack learning components. For example, washing school windows, serving Thanksgiving treats to the community, or building a swing set for children may seem to have limited learning potential. Indeed this may be true for some students, but these activities, which generally occur outside of structured class time, contribute to the overall sense of community. The fact that they are led or encouraged by faculty shows that senior learners consider them important, and the fact that they mix students with local citizens, mixing cultures and races, almost certainly ensures that some learning, if not about biology, occurs. In every instance, students are encouraged to write about their experiences, and discussion within the class takes place.

One student who participated in the swing building, and who also taught briefly in the primary school, wrote that he had a transforming experience, and immediately applied to Teach for America upon his return. Furthermore, several students have written or said that they realized partway through their stay at BERC that they were immersed in an entirely black cultural milieu, something novel to their experience, and that they had forgotten entirely about this fact after their first day, realizing on reflection that they had at least temporarily become color blind.

Examples of the Integration of Service and Other Learning Experiences

Biology classes offered through BERC represent the efforts of many different faculty from several different institutions. Thus, each class has its own graded requirements, its own research or learning focus, and its own approach to the role of experiential learning and service-learning.

Almost all classes at BERC, including biology classes, require students to maintain a journal. In some cases, the structure of the journal is relatively undefined, but most students have received written guidelines concerning this assignment. One approach that has been widely used is to require that the journal include a set of reflective essays on specific experiences (e.g., reflections on the program, island ecology from the point of view of an island resident). Another approach has been to require short but frequent descriptions of individual learning experiences in the form of "Learning

Logs." This approach lends itself well to reflection on service projects, and is described in more detail in the handout reproduced at the end of this chapter.[1]

Some classes require more structured essays, which may be written after a class returns home, drawing upon journal entries written in the field. In many cases, the titles, or at least the topics, of these essays are assigned. In some classes, one of the essays is in the form of a transcribed and annotated interview with one of the resource people who interacted with the group. Biology students are often encouraged (or sometimes required) to read classic accounts of exploration (e.g., *Voyage of The Beagle* or *The Malay Archipelago*) as examples of writing that integrate various aspects of the learning experience.

Most classes require a research project, taking the form of a formal paper, a slide show, a video production, or a website. Depending on the focus of the class, these projects might include reflection on the service aspects of the course. Past biology classes have yielded many projects on the physico-chemistry of blueholes, some of which have eventually become student presentations at regional meetings and several of which have been sent directly to the Bahamas government. Other projects have focused on the presentation of marine biology or ecology to primary or high school classes. A few recent projects have focused on the conch fishery or the role of the bonefish in the battle between developers and conservationists.

Some projects have even explored issues that may become future service projects. For example, one developed the idea of a bird-watching walk, and included species lists for each proposed stop on the walk, together with descriptions of habitat types and the behavioral ecology of the birds involved. This project led directly to a request from the local governing board for a set of interpretive and educational "stations" with pictorial billboards scattered throughout the area. Stations would focus attention on topics of ecological and community importance (e.g., the significance of mangroves, the life history of bonefish, why it is important to leave undersized lobsters alone, etc.). This concept stimulated discussion of possible snorkeling paths (with labels) and "mangrove walks" within the local community, suggesting one way in which the service and the learning can feed back upon each other.

Generalizing the Lessons of BERC

BERC is unusual, and possibly unique, among field stations. It was created with an enormous amount of trust and goodwill, and it continues to grow for these same reasons. Its central mission, providing logistical support to students and researchers studying the natural environments of Andros

Island, has only been strengthened by its tripartite governance. The community in which it is based is part of the base itself, not something Other. And much of the interaction between that community base and the other stakeholders, including the users of the facilities, involves some form of service, much of which results in learning, both about biological issues and about life.

The extent to which this approach is generally applicable remains to be seen. Many field stations, whether in the United States or elsewhere, could benefit from BERC's approach. Many biology students could also find their field experiences much richer if they knew that there were practical applications for their findings and that they were actually helping people through their activities, and if they felt that they were part of a community that was larger than their class. In the case of BERC, these things have been made possible through recognition of the issues that arise from the colonial aspects of fieldwork and conscious attempts to address and mitigate those issues before they became problems. Service-learning is a tool that has proven helpful to the enterprise itself and to the students and faculty who have engaged in it.

Note

1. Several George Mason University field classes require that students construct a portfolio of their learning experiences. The general nature of this portfolio is outlined in a set of handouts provided to the students, and individual faculty members modify this general outline as they see fit. The portfolio includes, among other things, a research project, a set of 10 reflective essays, a five-page transcribed interview with a resource person, and a set of learning logs.

Guide to the writing of "Learning Logs"

Randy Gabel, a mathematician at George Mason University, coined the term Learning Log. It's one of the graded aspects of the NCC class called The Natural World. Randy's original desire was to provide structure to student journals, and to push writers in the direction of completeness, rigorous description and evaluation of experience, and the physical discipline of regular writing. The log definition has been modified for our field classes, but the logs are still designed to help the learning process by:

Maintaining a complete description of all learning activities and occasions
Providing a regular opportunity for reflection on the meaning of experiences, and the relationships between experiences
Demanding the regular, more than daily, written recording of learning

Learning Logs for our classes will each have these components:

1. An **Abstract** describing the important aspects of the learning experience. For our purposes, the Abstract is written as prose, using sentences and a few paragraphs (as opposed to using fragments or bulleted statements). The abstract gives a brief explanation of what experiences occurred, and what evidence was relevant to the learning involved. For example, a poorly presented abstract might say that " cool things were discussed and there was a great picture....", while a well written abstract might say that "the speaker described the following anecdote that revealed what their life was like in the 1920's, and illustrated it with a photograph of them in their fishing boat with their crab traps...."

The abstract is not an opportunity to talk about your own emotions or opinions, unless you can support them with reference to the evidence you experienced. For example, it is not appropriate to simply say that you were bored, or grossed out, or felt really happy, without describing the evidence that made you feel this way. In general, this kind of personal information does not appear in an abstract.

The purpose of the abstract is to provide a clear, concise summary of the learning experience.

2. **A list of significant facts** that you will remember from this experience. This list can be done as a set of bulleted sentences, but make them full sentences. Some experiences will have a single key aspect, others will have two or more, but limit this list to the really important issues.

3. A similar **list of questions** that the experience raised. These might be issues that you were confused about, or observations that you made that might stimulate others to think about the topic. Think of these as discussion questions. Present them as complete sentences, and raise them whenever the group is discussing the experience.

4. Additions to a running **Glossary**. These additions should include any terms or concepts, together with their definitions, that the learning experience introduced you to. Include anything that is new to you, or that you learned to understand in a new or different way. If your

understanding of concepts or terms changes as time goes on, then simply redefine the term, and link your new definition with the older one (see the next component).

5. A representation of the connections between this experience and at least two others that you have had in this class (more if you want, but at least two). This representation can be entirely verbal or include a schematic. Remember to think about links with class readings, discussions, visits to physical resources like museums or parks, and interviews with human resource providers, including the faculty for the class. Make your explanation clear enough that your representation will have meaning for someone who was not part of this class (i.e., don't just reference "Tom" without giving enough information that a naïve reader could decipher who Tom is.

Write a learning log for each learning experience. If you don't know what a learning experience looks like, here are some examples:

Reading a book chapter
Reading a critical essay
Listening to a resource person
Talking with a resource person
Listening to a lecture or formal talk
Listening to a musical performance
Visiting a museum
Watching a play
Reading a poem
Participating in a group discussion about the day's activities
Participating in a church service
Participating in a community service project
Participating in lab, field or library research

In other words, just about any of the academic aspects of your class. By completing learning logs for each experience you have, you are preparing a complete record of your learning journey.

NB. You have a lot of freedom in determining the format of your Learning Log, as long as it contains all of these required parts. Probably the easiest way to make it comprehensible to your audience is to use headings (like Synopsis, Salient Facts, Important Questions, etc.). Page numbers will make it MUCH easier to understand the Links section if you are referencing other parts of the Log.

The final draft, included in your Portfolio, must be typed. This may require that you revisit your learning experience after your trip. So much the better- you'll remember all the great learning experiences you had while you type them up.

Biology and Service-Learning: Logical Links

by Joel H. Ostroff and David C. Brubaker

Edward Zlotkowski in "Does Service-Learning Have a Future?" (1995) asks whether there is a future for service-learning in America. At the 1996 and 1997 Dream and Design workshops held by the Florida Campus Compact, this question was explored in the plenary sessions from many perspectives. The resounding "yes" given by all of the disciplines present represented a clarion call to sustain service-learning as an essential component of college curricula.

Nowhere is this resolve more important than in both the biological sciences and the environmental/health sciences. Infusion of service-learning into the basic curricula of biological sciences is as manifestly important as is the need for biologists to become skilled in the realm of computer-based high technology. This area of study must expand service-learning into a universal curricular component that is interwoven throughout all of the biological subdisciplines. This is essential to prevent biology from becoming an insular science with little or no direct link to societal needs and responsibilities. We no longer can afford to sit in ivory-towered academic institutions isolated from the problems, promise, and interrelationships of the rest of human society. Biologists must be trained to maintain an active and involved presence in everyday life.

With the advent of the "new genetics" and the "second golden age of biology," this principle becomes even more critical. It is essential that upcoming biologists be taught social responsibility in light of the developments that continuously emerge from the new genetics, with its varied promises and threats. Molecular genetics has had an impact across every discipline of biology, from anatomy to embryology to ecology. Its effect on human welfare (e.g., the production of human insulin from bacterial sources [Raso 1998]), agricultural and domestic stock development (consider the current debate over Dolly the sheep and animal cloning [Wilmut 1998]), and the preservation and analysis of the world's ecosystems and species (Bryant 1998) brings promise of great benefits. At the same time, we are routinely reminded of the potential dangers irresponsible use can pose. Consider the furor over the threat to civilization from biological weapons of mass destruction that were apparently being developed in Iraq. In short, as biological and medical discoveries have increased, they have begun to pervade more and more aspects of our daily lives.

Currently offering benefits to the disenfranchised of this country, and someday perhaps to those of the world, service-learning provides avenues of connection and involvement for the disempowered and the underprivileged as formerly institutionally isolated academics find routes for disseminating biological gains to society at large. Furthermore, by humanizing and making socially accessible the core contents of biology courses, biologists foster a sense of respect and responsibility for the proper use of the scientific tools currently being developed. This in turn will help to reduce the chance that these discoveries will do general harm or provide benefit only to a wealthy few.

Relatedly, service-learning can play an important part in helping us rehumanize the often seemingly dehumanizing effects of high technology. While the ever-increasing availability and use of the Internet has opened enormous vistas for people around the globe, permitting electronic access to information on an unprecedented scale while creating literally world-wide communication opportunities, it has also created a significant venue for depersonalization and social isolation. As individuals connected with others only through the 'Net, we can become disembodied entities sitting alone at computer consoles with no personal stake in the outcomes of our computer-generated effects and no need to feel emotional ties to the other disembodied beings in our virtual universe. American society is already seeing an alarming increase in social disjunction, accompanied by a loss of morality, responsibility, and community connection among our youth. However, by incorporating service-learning into all aspects of our educational system, we can begin to take positive steps toward reinstituting those philosophies and principles of public responsibility upon which the American educational system was originally based. This is especially important for scientific education, since the general public view of science is of a self-contained undertaking indifferent to its effects on social welfare.

Indeed, with the ever-increasing influence of biology on our society, it is critically important that a humanizing of science and a recognition of biology's responsibilities to humanity be emphasized throughout all of its subdisciplines. Service-learning addresses biology's application in social environments and provides opportunities for social activity that inspires a scientific social consciousness. Too often students are given training in specific course content with little or no attention paid to the societal impacts of scientific discoveries or to the ways in which the content of a course could be utilized for social betterment. By incorporating service-learning into its pedagogy, biology will better train its students to become integral components of a better society — individuals able to contribute positively and beneficially to the world.

Still another benefit of service-learning in biology is the way in which it trains students to work effectively in public arenas, thereby deflecting the increasing impact of proponents of antiscience and pseudoscience — groups whose efforts help to undermine, negate, or even eliminate the benefits that biology and all the sciences can bring to humankind. By teaching our students social activism along with scientific knowledge, we will educate a generation intellectually armed and emotionally prepared to contribute to a more enlightened world. Service-learning, with its ability to clarify the role biology can play in creating such a world, will help to make our emerging biologists more than just effectively trained scientists. It will also make them true citizens.

But how are we, as biologists, to incorporate service-learning into the core of our already overburdened course curricula? The *why* of increasing service-learning in biology seems patently obvious. A more difficult question is *what* we need to do to accomplish this aim. Must we tear apart the very fabric of traditional biological education? Of course not! As biologists, and as educators, we must seek ways of integrating service-learning into our curricula in the least disruptive and most efficient manner possible.

Passing over at this point arguments as to whether service-learning should be a course requirement, an optional course track, or a supplemental extra-credit assignment, we wish to focus now on the various service-related areas that can be tapped by a biology class.

First, we must bear in mind that the success of service-learning projects is always a function of the openness, interest, and imagination of the instructor. If students are to be taught social utility, awareness, and activism, then their instructor must be prepared to think beyond the limits of the classroom and the laboratory. He or she must see how service-learning can be made adaptable to course content. If the instructor limits his or her personal imagination, students cannot learn to stretch theirs.

Implementation of service-learning, then, can be as simple as seeking out problem areas within the college or university community itself. Often a quick search of the school environs will manifest several problems of significance that can be integrated into the education of a biologist. For example, are there large retaining ponds on the school's grounds that need attention? Or would an energy usage survey and analysis be beneficial to conserve natural resources? What public health problems routinely impact the local community that also impact the college community? How can these be addressed?

Reaching beyond the confines of the campus into the general public vastly expands the opportunities for developing service-learning projects and identifying agencies needing and willing to accept student assistance. All that is required is a degree of attitudinal flexibility. After all, when viewed from a biological perspective, psychological issues clearly reflect a specialized form of animal behavior, while sociological issues can be viewed as aspects of population ecology with a specifically human focus. When the work of community agencies is viewed in this way, there is no shortage of opportunities of which faculty can avail themselves. Most often, even in relatively rural regions, more opportunities can be found than there will be students available to take advantage of them.

Admittedly, it is most effective to have a centralized service-learning office to assist with administrative and logistical needs, to act as a liaison between the instructor and community agencies, and to maintain and build a file of agency resources. Lack of such a center does not mean that service-learning cannot or should not be attempted, however. It simply limits an instructor's range of projects to those with which he or she is personally familiar.

Obviously, the public need for assistance with a vast array of issues will only continue to grow for the foreseeable future. The effects and influences of biology will also expand as new genetic discoveries are introduced, new medical issues arise, the population continues to age, and so on. As biology moves into more and more social arenas, the role of service-learning in biology courses must correspondingly increase.

The opening question of this essay was, Is there a future for service-learning in America? It seems to us that the question, from the standpoint of biology, should instead be, Is there a limit to the future application of service-learning in America (or even the world)? There is indeed a future for service-learning, and biology must serve as one essential key to its application, benefits, and expansion.

References

Bryant, Peter. (1998). *Biodiversity and Conservation: A Hypertextbook.* Irvine, CA: University of California-Irvine.

Raso, Jack. (1998). "The Future Is Now: The "Biopharm" Revolution." *American Council on Science and Health: Priorities* 10(1): 10.

Wilmut, Ian, et al. (February 1998). "A Flock of Clones." *Nature* 385(6619): 810-814.

Zlotkowski, Edward. (1995). "Does Service-Learning Have a Future?" *Michigan Journal of Community Service Learning* 2: 123-133.

Reprints From
Science and Society: Redefining the Relationship

Service-Learning and the Environment Meet at Clear Lake

Brevard Community College, Cocoa, Florida

The waters of Clear Lake, located on Brevard Community College's (BCC's) Cocoa campus, have long been utilized by both the students and the general public for a wide variety of activities. However, over the last three decades, water flow to the lake has been greatly altered. Most of the natural springs feeding the lake have been blocked, while drainage and runoff from surrounding BCC parking areas have been diverted into Clear Lake. Despite all of these important changes, the lake had not been tested to determine whether or not it was safe for human use.

Joel Ostroff, associate professor of microbiology at BCC, realized the potential risk to students and local residents. He decided to offer a service-learning component to his microbiology class in order to scientifically test the safety of Clear Lake's water. In addition, Barbara Thomas, assistant professor of environmental science, and Patricia Blaney, adjunct instructor, encouraged students from their classes to participate in the study of flora and fauna around the lake.

Participation in the service-learning program was optional. Those students who chose to participate were required to provide a minimum of 20 service hours at the lake, a final reflection paper indicating the student's overall impression of the experience, and mandatory attendance at a two-hour group reflection meeting. Students who fulfilled these requirements received 10 percent added to their total test score. Since test scores account for half the course grade, this "extra credit" generally raises a student's grade by half a letter. With this incentive, all 30 students in his microbiology course decided to participate. This was unexpected, as Ostroff had previously used the same motivation to participate in service-learning in another course and had achieved only 35 to 40 percent participation.

The BCC students were divided into teams of four to five students, and each team was assigned two to three students from the DRIVE (Deeds and Recreation Invalidate Violence Everywhere) program. DRIVE takes at-risk students from the local area and gives them opportunities they would not otherwise have. A total of 10 DRIVE students participated in the project.

First, Ostroff assigned a specific test site along the lake to each of the five teams. He then trained the BCC students in the use and maintenance of all the equipment and demonstrated all sampling, testing, and laboratory techniques. Each team was responsible for collection and analysis of its own water samples as well as documentation of all relevant data. Samples were tested for pH, temperature, dissolved oxygen, carbon dioxide, nitrates, phosphates, E. coli, and total coliforms. The students completed 15 testing objectives by participating in this project. Once the BCC students were comfortable with their own abilities, they began training the DRIVE participants in all facets of the testing process.

Two students from Blaney's class and two students from Thomas's class worked with other DRIVE students to collect plant and animal specimens from around the lake. Plants and animals were identified, and a species record of the lake's flora and fauna was created. This will be useful as a comparison and reference guide for any studies done in the future.

After final analysis of all data, it was determined that Clear Lake was highly polluted with bacteria. Although the lake was still safe for most animals and plants, it was deemed "unsafe" for humans. As a direct result of these findings, the college will no longer hold school events that encourage swimming in the lake. Administrative decisions concerning a cleanup of the lake are still pending.

Ostroff plans to continue this study in the future, using the same basic structure but incorporating additional chemical tests. All data acquired throughout this project have been documented, graphed, and permanently recorded on computer disk. As this project becomes a permanent part of the microbiology course, the repeated monitoring of these chemical levels will provide an ongoing history of the lake's vitality.

The positive effects of optional service-learning on his students are particularly encouraging to Ostroff. He believes that mandatory service-learning detracts from the potential benefits. However, he has discovered that most students get very excited about the project once they decide to involve themselves, and that this motivates them to work even harder in class. This project was particularly effective because the service-learning option so closely paralleled the classroom course content. The students were able to put into actual practice many of the techniques they had been hearing about throughout the semester. This additional familiarity and understanding of the concepts introduced in the course generally afford the service-learning students a significant advantage as far as overall test grades are concerned. Ostroff plans to write an article for publication using statistics from college-wide service-learning classes that show increased classroom performance from those students participating in service-learning.

Contact: Joel Ostroff, Ostroff_ J@Al.Brevard.cc.FL.US

Gardening for Humanity

Chandler-Gilbert Community College, Chandler, Arizona

In 1984, the town of Gilbert, Arizona, built six water retention ponds used to percolate purified wastewater back into the groundwater table. Nine years later, in 1993, Gilbert was awarded a Heritage grant by the Arizona Game and Fish Department to help design and implement an urban wildlife enhancement plan for the water recharge site. The site being only a few years old, Pushpa Ramakrishna, along with other faculty members at Chandler-Gilbert Community College, decided that the new site provided an opportunity for students to enhance the beauty of their surroundings while studying the safety and natural resources of the site.

Ramakrishna involved 48 students from her introductory course, Biology Concepts, and 48 students from her upper-level course intended for majors, General Biology.

In both classes, students were broken up into small groups of four to five students to study one of four topics in depth. Those topics were global warming and the greenhouse effect, water pollution, plant and tree diversity, and birds and their migratory patterns.

The small groups from both classes went to the site once during the semester. All the groups studying a specific topic went together, so a total of four visits were made to the site over the course of the semester. At the site, students focusing on global warming and the greenhouse effect planted more trees and plants. Those focusing on water pollution tested the water for oxygen content, presence of fecal matter, hardness, temperature, and pH. The information was given to the Town of Gilbert Reclamation Plant, which had never tested water quality in the retention ponds that retain water after running through the purifiers. This information will be the basis for an ongoing study by Ramakrishna's class, and as more information is gathered, her classes will begin to analyze the changes in the data. Those students studying plant and tree diversity used books and keys to identify different plants and trees. Again, this information was given to the site as a record. The students studying birdlife used binoculars and books to identify at least 15 varieties of birds in the area, some of which had flown in from Alaska and Canada for the Arizona winter heat.

The students in Ramakrishna's lower-level course went to the site that one time, and then wrote a reflection paper on the experience. For students in her upper-level biology class, though, the service-learning project was one-third of their grade, and they continued to work on the project. As soon as they returned from their visit to the site, they started researching a paper on their expert topics.

While each group had different projects at the water reclamation site, back in the classroom each student met with a student from each of the other three groups and shared project results. As the students shared their projects with one another back in the classroom, they prepared bulletin boards and activities to teach their newfound knowledge to 45 children from a local boys and girls club attending Earth Week activities at the water reclamation site. Earth Week activities lasted Thursday, Friday, and Saturday. Students from Ramakrishna's course had to mentor one of the three days. The children visited the different booths to learn about different aspects of the environment, then got to do hands-on activities such as planting bean seeds in cups, testing water, identifying birds with binoculars, looked for microbes in water, and other similar activities. In addition, students from CGCC and the boys and girls club planted shrubs at the reclamation site during these days. The next day the students opened the project to the public, and many attended.

In addition, during their visits to the site, students helped to plant 800 trees that had been donated to the site but needed to be planted. Each group of four to five students planted approximately 25 to 30 plants and trees.

Ramakrishna also created a website for the class and has listed the details of her course there. The website also contains the final research papers from the students and student comments on the project. The website address is <http://www.cgc.maricopa.edu/.ACADEMICWeb/biology/ecology.html>.

Ramakrishna was also aided by Ben Newman. Every Chandler-Gilbert class with a significant service-learning component is given a service-learning assistant. Service-learning assistants meet every week in a general meeting with other service-learning assistants and also attend workshops. Newman helped with the paperwork and making arrangements for the project. Ramakrishna plans to continue the course in the future, using the same format. As the data collections grow from repeated testings, she will bring more analysis into the service-learning project as well. Chemistry professor Chuck Bedall and mathematics professor Melinda Radibaugh are also developing related service-learning projects at the water reclamation site, and collaboration between their courses is likely in the future.

Contact: Pushpa Ramakrishna, Ramakrishna@cgc.maricopa.edu

A Pilot Project to Teach Basic Botany to Fifth Graders

Arizona State University, Tempe, Arizona

Diann Peart, the education coordinator for Arizona State University's (ASU's) Department of Botany, has just completed the first year of a proposed four-year mentoring program for local middle school students. Students enrolled in Plants and Society, an introductory botany course for nonmajors, had the option of participating in the botany service-learning internship, which works in conjunction with the Plants and Society course. Students who participate in the botany service-learning internship attend the same three–credit hour lecture and one–credit hour laboratories as the other botany students. In addition, they also enroll in an additional three–credit hour internship specifically designated as service-learning. With this arrangement, the faculty teaching the botany class do not have to be involved in the service-learning portion of the class. It is completely run by Peart, Nancy Crocker, a part-time service-learning facilitator last year, and a botany department teaching assistant.

The program began with the planting of two gardens, one at the Julian Middle School campus, one on the ASU campus. ASU botany service-learning has become the heart of the Julian science curriculum. Gloria Henderson, principal of Julian Middle School, realizing the long-term commitment Peart was planning to make, invited the ASU program into the classroom. Previously, Julian students received little training in the sciences.

Throughout the school year, a class of fifth graders were bused from Julian to the ASU garden site every Tuesday. On Thursday mornings, service-learning interns from ASU commuted to the garden at the middle school. When in the garden, ASU service-learning interns were implementing concepts learned in their Plants and Society lectures and labs, modifying them for the fifth graders. The gardens are kept year round to facilitate the understanding of extended life cycles of certain plants. In addition, Peart purchased Wisconsin Fast-Plant Kits, which illustrate the entire life cycle of plants. She used these kits so that the fifth graders could see at least one life cycle of the plants before they left for summer break. Since the ASU service-learning interns take the botany course for only one semester and cannot repeat the course for credit, the first group of tutors left at the end of the semester, and a new group of tutors joined second semester. The continuing factor in the gardens became the fifth graders, who, having learned about the garden, were eager to introduce the new tutors to their garden.

A weekly one-hour planning session was held and facilitated by Crocker. This was helpful in carrying out the logistics of the program and answering questions from the interns. Much of the reflection on the garden activities took place on ASU's Electronic Forum (EF), a computer conferencing program that allows interns to participate in discussion from distant sites and at hours convenient to their schedules. It was also convenient for grading, since EF monitors the time spent on the system and what students read and post. Students were required to post on EF at least twice a week.

These postings were used in three ways. Students had reading assignments for the class, and their postings reflected their responses to the material. Students were also required to reflect on how their mentoring of the fifth graders was proceeding. These postings were accessible to all other service-learning interns. The final task interns performed on EF was to respond to a fellow student's posting. These responses were also available to the entire class; one student could then respond to another student's response. Peart notes that a substantial dialogue was created on the system and that, in time, students came to enjoy working with EF, seeing it as a vital part of their curriculum.

Course grades for the service-learning interns were determined by Peart, Crocker, and the botany teaching assistant for the course. They all read and discussed the EF postings and on-site participation, and reviewed the interns' work with the Julian students.

The program was a tremendous success its first year, and while the ASU arboretum staff inadvertently uprooted the ASU garden, the Julian garden increased to the size of a volleyball court and is still alive and well. As the service-learning mentoring program moves into its second year, it is expanding rapidly. Next year, all fifth-grade classes at Julian Middle School will participate in the garden, as well as a few students from this year's course who did not want to leave the garden. This means an increase from 25 students mentored this year to around 60 next year.

In addition, as this year's pilot group moves into the sixth grade, all of the sixth graders at Julian will participate in science service-learning. In the sixth-grade year, the program will teach students physical geography, with service-learning interns from an introductory geography lab providing the tutoring. In future years, the seventh grade will be provided with tutoring in ecology and conservation, and the eighth grade will be tutored in environmental geology. All corresponding ASU service-learning interns will work from linked courses to teach these various science lessons, and will follow the same structure as the initial science class, Plants and Society.

Next year, the science service-learning project will also start a garden on the nearby Salt River Pima-Maricopa Indian Community. The tribe is very supportive, and elders from the tribe have asked whether they can garden with their children and teach them the names of the plants in their language. They have been welcomed. Crocker asked a tribal elder what the children would be interested in growing, and he expressed an interest in chilies. Various projects can be done with the chilies, but some will be sold at the local museum, with profits returning to enlarge and enhance the garden and the museum. As the program grows, it is planned that the same science service-learning mentoring program that was piloted at Julian will be implemented at the school on the Salt River reservation.

Peart also has long-term plans for the project, plans she hopes will make all of these projects self-sustaining. When the Julian students complete eighth grade, she wants to take them to a camp owned by ASU in the mountains. There, in a four-week course, the importance of mentoring will be outlined, and teaching methods will be explored. The hope is to prepare the students to start mentoring when they move on to high school. So, in the ninth grade, they would mentor with fifth graders in the garden, just as they were once mentored by ASU service-learning interns. And in the tenth grade, they would mentor the sixth graders in physical geography, and so on until they graduate. The science service-learning project would be self-sustaining, with students who were once tutored now providing the tutoring. ASU, meanwhile, would continue the project at other schools, creating self-sustaining programs in other places. Peart notes that it is always important to add a cyclical element to all projects so that the community helped eventually helps itself, and can sustain the project without need for outside support.

Since word of her long-term plans has started to circulate, Peart has more requests than she can fill and many leads to follow. She stresses that the project thus far has required very little funding for development, an attractive component for any program. She also notes that the program has evolved tremendously since its planning stages, and that its success has been due to flexibility in building the project as it goes.

Contact: Diann Peart, AODEP@asuvm.inre.asu.edu

Summary Course Descriptions

Aquatic Biology Laboratory, Case Western Reserve University

In the Aquatic Biology Laboratory (Biol 339), students are introduced to standard sampling techniques and analysis, and are given the opportunity to complete two major projects. The first is an analysis of the community structure in ponds at our biological field station. The second utilizes a service-learning approach in conjunction with the Audubon Society of Greater Cleveland. Three years ago, we were asked to survey a pond in one of the Society's sanctuaries. For the last two years, we have been working on a wetland on another of its sanctuaries that is threatened by development in the watershed. Two years ago, we were asked to survey the biological aspects of the wetland to begin a species list for the property. Last year, we focused on the hydrology of the system by building a high/low water-level indicator, determining the physical parameters of the inflow and outflows, conducting an analysis of the water table, and measuring precipitation levels. The hydrology is of particular concern to the Audubon Society, because there is a major question whether the aquifer can support the additional 250 wells proposed by the development. Some of the data we generated have been used in discussions by the Audubon Society with developers and city planners.

    Contact: Jim Bader, Department of Biology, Case Western Reserve University, 10900 Euclid Avenue, Cleveland, OH 44106, 70Hjxbl4@po.cwru.edu

To Feed The World, Seattle University

To Feed the World is an interdisciplinary course offered to all Seattle University students at the junior/senior level. It satisfies the interdisciplinary requirement of the university core curriculum. The course content focuses on the history of human food production and distribution methods from the time of the agricultural revolution to the present. The course introduces students to the interplay of biology, ecology, economics, culture, and politics in the production and distribution of food in a complicated world. The service-learning component of the class provides students with experiential learning at the community level and assists them in making the connection between local issues of hunger and disenfranchisement in Seattle with those same issues at the global level. Students are required to work two hours per week (20 hours total) at preselected agencies. Some of the agencies are Northwest Harvest, Chicken Soup Brigade, and St. James Family Kitchen. Students keep a "guided journal" of their service and share their experiences and reflections during several class discussions. Their journal is in part a record of their service, the people they meet, and their reactions on their service and their teaming. It is enhanced by a weekly series of "guided questions" that both anticipate where the students are in their personal experience and ask them to connect what they learn to the class content. The final question asks students to reflect on how the skills they have learned are enhanced during their service project and to write a personal goals statement.

Contact: David C. Brubaker, Associate Professor of Biology, Department of Biology, Seattle University, Seattle, WA 98122, ph 206/296-5485, bru@seattleu.edu

Introduction to Ecological Systems, Seattle University

Introduction to Ecological Systems is a required sophomore course for ecological studies majors. It is a field-oriented course introducing students to the major ecosystems of the Pacific Northwest. It uses a natural history approach, which incorporates a day-long field trip to each ecosystem, followed by a review session each week. Students keep a natural history field journal, which is a collection of their field notes, interpretations, reflections, species lists, and species write-ups. The service-learning component is designed to introduce students to how people in the community use ecological knowledge either to restore or enhance their local ecosystems or to inform themselves and their children about environmental issues. Students are required to complete a 20-hour community service project with preselected community groups, nonprofit agencies, or local government agencies. The projects range from stream or pond restoration, native plant salvage, and plant community surveys for a wetlands to developing environmental educational materials for local schools, parks, and recreation programs. Students keep a journal of their activities, the people they meet, and their reflections on their service, and share them in several class discussions. Weekly "guided questions" encourage students to connect their service projects with course material and their personal development.

Contact: David C. Brubaker, Associate Professor of Biology, Department of Biology, Seattle University, Seattle, WA 98122, ph 206/296-5485, bru@ seattleu.edu

Honors Biology, Virginia Tech

Honors Biology (H12-05, H12-06) is very nontraditional in that there are no lectures. One day a week students are online from their dormitory rooms solving problems and helping one another understand biology. The second day they are in class collaboratively working on new questions. The third day they listen to outside speakers, most of whom are not biologists. Service-learning is an important component of the class: I believe that we learn subject matter best when we teach it. This course has three levels of student interaction that promote learning through teaching. At one level, upper-class students who have had Honors Biology are online tutoring students currently taking the class. At a second level, students in the class are randomly assigned to peer-critique another student's work. At the third level, students in Honors Biology are linked online with high school students located in another part of the state, helping high school students learn biology.

Contact: Arthur L. Buikema, Jr., Professor of Ecology, Environmental Science, Evolution, and Systematics, Virginia Polytechnic Institute and State University, Blacksburg, VA 24060-0406, ph 540/231-5180, buik@vt.edu

Topics in Biology, Thomas More College

Topics in Biology (BIO 355) is also known as the CORRE (Center for Ohio River Research and Education) docent program. Students (a.k.a. the docents) use their knowledge and skills in biology to develop and present their own scientifically significant and educationally fulfilling field trip program to visiting groups of students in elementary and secondary education. Docents spend the first part of the semester developing a 30- to 40-minute presentation on a particular topic that is relevant to the CORRE and adaptable to the needs of students in grades 3 to 5, 6 to 9, and 10 to 12. The latter part of the semester is spent conducting the field trips, which involve hands-on participation as well as discussion. The docents keep a reflection log that summarizes and reflects on the most successful aspects and the less than perfect aspects of the presentation. Through this course, students are providing a service to the schools in the community while at the same time growing in ways that the traditional classroom cannot provide by putting their knowledge and skills to the test.

Contact: John Hageman, Associate Professor of Biology, Director of CORRE, Thomas More College, Crestview Hills, KY 41017, ph 606/635-6941 (CORRE), john.hageman@thomasmore.edu

Modern Molecular Genetics, Technology, and Society, University of Notre Dame

Modern Molecular Genetics, Technology, and Society (BIOS 110) is intended for freshman nonscience majors who have a general interest in human genetics. The course objectives are to educate students on the relatively new field of molecular genetics and to discuss the social and ethical implications of genetic technology. The service-learning opportunity is available to any student in the course. Students carry out one of the following projects with the Logan Center, a regional center for people with genetic and congenital disorders: (1) prepare a packet of information on a genetic condition for families whose children are born with the disorder; (2) work in the Logan School to aid teachers; (3) work as a helper to a Logan family who has a child with a disability; (4) work in the Best Buddies program or the Socialization program, which allows one-on-one contact with a Logan client. The service project takes the place of one exam and requires at least 10 hours of service work during the semester. The project also requires a daily journal, attendance at two debriefing sessions run by the Logan volunteer coordinator, and a reflection paper.

Contact: Michelle A. Murphy, Professor, Cell Biology and Genetics Laboratory, Department of Biological Sciences, University of Notre Dame, Notre Dame, IN 46556, ph 219/631-9343, Michelle.A.Murphy.20@nd.edu

Environment and Life, Indiana University East

The service-learning components in my course Environment and Life (L108) are centered on environmental themes. Environment and Life is a course restricted to nonscience majors where 60 students per semester become familiar with the role of science in addressing environmental concerns. Course objectives include (1) a survey of how humans manage and use the environment; (2) an understanding of the forces operating in ecosystems and how they are affected by human activities; (3) development of communication, critical-thinking, and problem-solving skills; and (4) an appreciation of the historical, intellectual, cultural, economic, and ethical perspectives on environmental issues. I have incorporated a service-learning option into a required environmental project in this course. The project is designed to allow students to investigate ecological and sociological principles involved in deciding how natural resources are used. This process is examined as being representative of biologic and social forces affecting resource use on global scales. I require that projects deal with an environmental problem where biological and sociological concepts covered in class are applicable, and that they offer solutions to the problem that are sensitive to the perspectives of affected parties (some solutions must involve immediate action that the group or classmates can take). Service projects are strongly encouraged because (1) they deal with solving local environmental problems, (2) collaborating with a contact person/supervisor at an organization models the real process of environmental problem solving, (3) students learn the needs and concerns of organizations that deal with environmental issues and provide a service that helps meet those needs, and (4) students have done something and develop feelings of empowerment.

Contact: Neil Sabine, Associate Professor of Biology, Department of Natural Science and Mathematics, Indiana University East, Richmond, IN 47374, ph 765/973-8389, nsabine@indiana.edu

Argument in Scientific Writing, University of Colorado

Argument in Scientific Writing (EPOB 3940) prepares upper-division science students for academic and professional writing, including proposal writing and research publication. Whereas many students write research proposals and publications that advance their own work, other students need project material in order to practice their growing skills. Service-learning projects provide that material while enabling students to offer a valuable community service. Students may choose from two options: (1) writing research papers and/or proposals for nonprofit science organizations or K-12 science teachers, or (2) working for the organization or teacher in other ways and using the experience and information as a basis for their writing. Not only does this approach give students invaluable experience with real situations and applied scientific work, allow them to work with professionals in fields of interest, and teach them about community dynamics; it also enables them to appreciate the practical value of their writing skills as they gain thousands of dollars for K-12 science education and participate in publications for science nonprofits.

Contact: Sally Susnowitz, Senior Instructor, Department of Environmental, Population, and Organismic Biology, University of Colorado, Boulder, CO 80309-0334, ph 303/492-4345, Sally.Susnowitz@Colorado.edu

Appendix

Suggested Readings

Ageles, Tom P. (1973). "Environmental Education: A Community/University Approach." *Journal of College Science Teaching* 3(1): 50-53.

Boyte, Harry D. (June 1991). "Community Service and Civic Education." *Phi Delta Kappan* 72(10): 765-768.

Bringle, Robert G. (November/December 1997). "Service-Learning in Higher Education." *Journal of Higher Education* 68(6): 715-717.

Burns, Lenard T. (October 1998). "Make Sure It's *Service-Learning*, Not Just Community Service." *Education Digest* 64(2): 38-41.

Chadbourne, Joseph H. (1974). *The Ohio Watershed Heritage Project. An Environmental Community Service for Secondary School Students.* Cleveland, OH: Institute for Environmental Education.

Chapin, June R. (September/October 1998). "Is Service-Learning a Good Idea? Data From the National Longitudinal Study of 1998." *Social Studies* 89(5): 205-211.

Conrad, D., and K. Hedin. (June 1991). "School-Based Community Service: What We Know From Research and Theory." *Phi Delta Kappan* 72(10): 743-750.

Fiffer, Steve, and Sharon Sloan Fiffer. (1994). *Fifty Ways to Help Your Community: A Handbook for Change.* New York, NY: Doubleday.

Gardner, Bonnie. (September 1997). "The Controversy Over Service-Learning." *NEA Today* 16(2): 17.

Gose, Ben. (November 14, 1997). "Many Colleges Move to Link Courses With Volunteerism." *The Chronicle of Higher Education*: A45-A46.

Greenberg, Jerrold S. (November/December 1997). "Service-Learning in Health Education." *Journal of Health Education* 28(6): 345-349.

James, Howard G. (1973). "School and Community Involvement in a High School Biology Museum." *Science Teacher* 40(7): 42-44.

Laetsch, W.M., and Robert C. Knott. (1981). *Outdoor Biology Instructional Strategies (OBIS): 1972-79. Final Project Report.* Washington, DC: National Science Foundation.

Serow, R. (1991). "Students and Voluntarism: Looking Into the Motive of Community Service Participation." *American Educational Research Journal* 28(3): 543-556.

Sewall, Angela Maynard. (Summer 1997). "Serving to Learn and Learning to Serve." *National Forum* 77(3): 3-4.

Silcox, Harry. (1993). *A How-To Guide to Reflection: Adding Cognitive Learning to Community Service Programs.* Holland, PA: Brighton Press.

Zamm, Michael, et al. (1990). *Training Student Organizers Curriculum.* Rev. ed. New York, NY: Council on the Environment of New York City.

Contributors to This Volume

Volume Editors

David C. Brubaker
Associate Professor of Biology
Seattle University
Department of Biology, Seattle, WA 98122
bru@seattleu.edu

Joel H. Ostroff
Professor Emeritus of Microbiology, Brevard Community College
(Currently) Southwestern Community College
447 College Drive, Sylva, NC 28779
JOstroff@southwest.cc.nc.us

Contributors

Amal Abu-Shakra
Assistant Professor
North Carolina Central University
Durham, NC 27707
Abushak@wpo.nccu.edu

Paul D. Austin
Assistant Professor
Azusa Pacific University
Department of Biological Sciences, Azusa, CA 91702
PAustin@APUNET.APU.EDU

A. Christine Brown
Assistant Professor of Life Sciences
University of New England
Department of Life Sciences, University Hills Beach Road,
    Biddeford, ME 04005
Sbrown@mailbox.UNE.edu

Luther Brown
Associate Professor of Integrative Studies and Biology
New Century College
George Mason University
Fairfax, VA 22030
Lbrow4@gmu.edu

John C. Kennell
James Trustee Assistant Professor of Biological Sciences
Southern Methodist University
Department of Biological Sciences, Dallas, TX 75275-0376
jkennel@mail.smu.edu

Scott S. Kinnes
Assistant Professor
Azusa Pacific University
Department of Biological Sciences, Azusa, CA 91702
Skinnes@APUNET.APU.Edu

Peter Lortz
Instructor in Biology and Program Director, Service-Learning in
    the Natural Sciences
North Seattle Community College
Seattle, WA 98103
plortz@seaccd.ctc.edu

Samuel A. McReynolds
Associate Professor of Social and Behavioral Sciences
University of New England
Department of Social Sciences, University Hills Beach Road,
    Biddeford, ME 04005
SmcReynolds@mailbox.une.edu

Tun Kyaw Nyein
Assistant Professor
North Carolina Central University
Department of Biology, Durham, NC 27707

Nancy K. Prentiss
Lecturer in Biology
University of Maine at Farmington
Department of Natural Sciences, 39 High Street, Farmington, ME 04938-1987
Prentiss@MAINE.MAINE.EDU

Alan Raflo
Research Associate
Virginia Polytechnic Institute and State University
Virginia Water Resources Research Center, 10 Sandy Hall,
    Blacksburg, VA 24061
araflo@vt.edu

Marianne Robertson
Assistant Professor of Biology
Milliken University
Department of Biology, Decatur, IL 62522-2084
mRobertson@mail.milliken.edu

Jeffrey A. Simmons
Assistant Professor of Biology and Environmental Sciences
West Virginia Wesleyan College
Department of Biology and Environmental Sciences,
    Buckhannon, WV 26201-2995
Simmons@WVWC.edu

Series Editor

Edward Zlotkowski is professor of English and was founding director of the Service-Learning Project at Bentley College. He is also senior associate at the American Association for Higher Education.

About AAHE

AAHE's Vision AAHE envisions a higher education enterprise that helps all Americans achieve the deep, lifelong learning they need to grow as individuals, participate in the democratic process, and succeed in a global economy.

AAHE's Mission AAHE is the individual membership organization that promotes the changes higher education must make to ensure its effectiveness in a complex, interconnected world. The association equips individuals and institutions committed to such changes with the knowledge they need to bring them about.

About AAHE's Series on Service-Learning in the Disciplines

The Series goes beyond simple "how to" to provide a rigorous intellectual forum. *Theoretical essays* illuminate issues of general importance to educators interested in using a service-learning pedagogy. *Pedagogical essays* discuss the design, implementation, conceptual content, outcomes, advantages, and disadvantages of specific service-learning programs, courses, and projects. All essays are authored by teacher-scholars in that discipline.

Representative of a wide range of individual interests and approaches, the Series provides substantive discussions supported by research, course models in a rich conceptual context, annotated bibliographies, and program descriptions.

Visit AAHE's website (www.aahe.org) for the list of disciplines covered in the Series, pricing, and ordering information.